Mazal Tov Tony on your Jerusalem Bar Mitzvah
14/5/14

May God Bless you Always
In All Ways

Rabbi Jay

Off The Wall

An anthology of
humorous anecdotes, episodes
and tidbits from the Synagogue,
Weddings, Funerals and
Bar/Bat Mitzvah

Rabbi Jay Karzen
Jerusalem's Bar Mitzvah King

Illustrations: Pepe Fainberg
Design and cover photographs: Mike Horton

ISBN 965-222-928-8

©
All rights reserved by
RITUALS UNLIMITED
email: jkarzen@netvision.net.il
Fax: 011-972-2-5672068
1999

```
Canadian Cataloguing in Publication Data

Karzen, Jay.
  Off the wall

  ISBN 1-55212-309-X

  1. Jewish wit and humor.  2. Rabbis--Humor.  I. Title.
  PN6231.J5K37 1999         818'.5402 C99-911288-0
```

TRAFFORD

This book was published *on-demand* **in cooperation with Trafford Publishing.**
On-demand publishing is a unique process and service of making a book available for retail sale to the public taking advantage of on-demand manufacturing and Internet marketing.
On-demand publishing includes promotions, retail sales, manufacturing, order fulfilment, accounting and collecting royalties on behalf of the author.

Suite 6E, 2333 Government St., Victoria, B.C. V8T 4P4, CANADA
Phone   250-383-6864   Toll-free   1-888-232-4444 (Canada & US)
Fax   250-383-6804   E-mail   sales@trafford.com
Web site   www.trafford.com   TRAFFORD PUBLISHING IS A DIVISION OF TRAFFORD HOLDINGS LTD.
Trafford Catalogue #99-0012   www.trafford.com/robots99-0012.html

Off The Wall

Rabbi Jay Karzen, of Jerusalem, Israel, is a native of Chicago, Illinois and was ordained at the Hebrew Theological College, Skokie, Illinois. Before his Aliyah to Israel in 1985, he served pulpits in Ottumwa and Council Bluffs, Iowa (1959-65) and for 22 years served as the spiritual leader of the prestigious Maine Township Jewish Congregation Shaare Emet, Des Plaines, Illinois. In the Chicagoland community he was active in many organizations. He was president of the Alumni Association of the HTC Yeshiva and served as Chairman of both the Radio/Television Broadcasting Commission of the Chicago Board of Rabbis and the Brit Milah/Ritual Circumcision Committee of the Chicago Rabbinical Council. He was the Jewish Chaplain of the Variety Club of Illinois.

In 1985, after emigrating to Israel, he founded Rituals Unlimited and serves as its president and director. RU is the largest Bar/Bat Mitzvah and Simcha Service in Jerusalem.

Tourists from literally all over the world avail themselves of his services. The Jerusalem Post referred to him as the "Bar Mitzvah King". As a volunteer, he also runs the Cemetery and Bereavement Program of the Association of Americans and Canadians in Israel (AACI)

Rabbi Karzen is married to the former Ruby Ray (noted Jerusalem interior designer) and is the father of 2 children and 10 grandchildren

Lovingly and Reverently
dedicated in memory of
our late beloved parents of
blessed memory
Max and Yetta Karzen
and
Israel and Minnie & Rose Ray

Contents

Foreword	15
Preface	18
A Poem	20

Rabbi Jay's World of Humor

The Address Of The Kotel	21
The Dancing Boys	22
We Vote For No Tefilin	25
The Spooky Bar Mitzvah	27
The Wrong Torah Portion	28
Other Wrong Parsha Stories	29
The "God Loves Humming" Bar Mitzvah	31
The "Start Me Off" Bar Mitzvah	32
The Baseball Bat Bat Mitzvah	34
The CD Rom Bar Mitzvah	37
The Priest And The Tefilin	38
The Bread & Wine Bar Mitzvah	40
The All in Hebrew Bar Mitzvah	40
Rosh Chodesh	41
Don't Make It Too Tight!	43
Peaking Too Soon	44
Good-Better-Best!	44
The Sentimental Tattered Talit	45
What Happened To The Tzitzit?	46
Forgetting The Melody	46
And What's Inside The Tefilin?	47
Teen Usherettes	48
The Woman Rabbi And The Talit	48
All Of A Sudden	49
The Mashiach In The Kitchen	50

On What Day Will The Messiah Arrive?	50
Praying To Phyllis	51
The Movie & CNN Crew	52
VIPs At The Bar Mitzvah	53
The No-Show Bar Mitzvah	54
The Conservative Talit?	55
The Partner	57
The Cellphone: A Call From On High	58
Tear Gas At Kotel	58
Adult Bar Mitzvah	59
The Three Generational Bar Mitzvah	61
The Hawaiian Bar Mitzvah	62
Funny E-mail And Faxes: No More Snail Mail	64
Sam Orbaum's Masterpiece In The Jerusalem Post	72
Taxi To Kotel	76
The Kotel Policeman And The Cellphone	78
The UJA Group And Netilat Yadayim	80
The Lady & The Mechitza	81
"Korim" In The Great Synagogue	82
Children's Creative Biblical Insights	83
Karzen vs. Richard Tucker	84
Chief Rabbi At Age 25	86
What? Me Make Mistakes In The Torah Reading?	86
Praying For Strawberries	87
The Cinerama Prayerbook	89
Questions Asked By Non-Jews	90
Merry Xmas, Rabbi!	92
My First Funeral Blunder	92
The Electric Spinning Rooftop Draydel	93
Tuesday Night At The Movies	94
The "Bluffer" Rebbe	95
Kelev, The Dog, Is Dead!	96
Tying The Knot & Going To The Dogs	97
The Oneg Tuesday Prison Caper	98

Having A Ball In Beersheba	100
Netanya's Chassidic Paradise	101
Hava Nagila At Yad Vashem	102
De "Plainer" Rebbe	103
I Am Triplets	103
Home Of Joyous Jewishness	104
A NOOJ	105
House Calls Can Be Dangerous	106
Beware Of 23rd Psalm In Winter	107
Funeral Melodies	108
The Cantor Does A Shereleh	108
Al & Millie Ruderman	109
Father & Son Do The Cemetery Circuit	109
Believe It Or Not Funeral Tidbits	110
The Family Feud: Rabbi, Do Something!	111
The White Envelope	112
The Taxidermist Request	113
Just Me At The Unveiling	114
How Many Make A Minyan?	115
This Is My Shul Because...	117
The Synagogue Janitorial Staff	118
The Only Rabbi In History To Be Thrown Out Of Saks	119
Jews By Choice Stories	121
Gerut (Conversion) Nachas Notes	126
"Selling" The First Born Sons	126
When Do Services Begin?	127
The Sermon Sleeper	128
The Saga of Page 335	129
The Bigger The Better	130
Non-Kosher Tape Recording	130
Creative Hebrew (?) Names	131
Hagbaah Lessons	132
Accidents Do Occur	134
Exodus to The Restroom	135

Noy or Goy?	136
"Shlepping" Nachas	136
Where Is The Loyalty?	138
JME & The Power Of The Mezuzah	139
Rabbis Make Babies Like Everyone Else	141
The Frail Groom	141
Concentrated To Me...	142
My Saddest Wedding	143
Squishing To The Chuppah	145
Boin	146
Rabbi Jay's Bar Mitzvah Day	148
KARZENISMS	150
GLOSSARY	152

Foreword

This anthology of humorous anecdotes, episodes, narratives and other happenings is a compilation of material spanning forty years of a rewarding rabbinical career in both the United States and now in Israel.

In these trying times, there is a desperate need for more daily laughter— or at least a good smile. The news we listen to on radio/television and read in the newspapers is heavy and often depressing. A friend, commenting on this phenomenon, told me that he religiously listens to the daily 7:00 AM English news and then the rest of the day is all downhill. It shouldn't have to be! Humor is a powerful antidote for despair and depression. The ability to laugh and appreciate the humor in the most absurd events of life, ought not be underestimated.

"OFF THE WALL" is a modest attempt to provide some much needed doses of humor. These TRUE stories have been shared with family and friends at the Shabbat table in both countries. Invariably, one of the listeners would urge me to publish these hilarious experiences so that a wider audience would be able to enjoy them and have a good laugh.

The obvious apocryphal story comes to mind of the Rabbi who had delivered a masterful sermon. At the Kiddush/collation, following services, an appreciative regular worshipper approached the Rav and congratulated him on yet another inspiring Dvar Torah.

"You must publish your words so that others can be inspired", she suggested. The Rabbi, in his modesty, replied: "Perhaps someday they will be published— posthumously!" "Well then", she retorted, "let's hope it's real soon!" Rather than wait, I have opted to seize the initiative and share these tidbits— sooner, rather than later.

I am grateful to the many cherished friends and neighbors who have listened to me relate these tidbits over the years, and who urged me to share them via the printed word. They have inspired this volume.

A very special thank you and "Yasher Koach" to my beloved "first wife" (that keeps her on her toes!) and life partner, Ruby, who gives of herself with boundless love and has an infectious enthusiasm for life. She has made these over four decades truly exciting as my beloved rabbinic-team partner and soulmate. I am eternally indebted to her for so very much..... not the least for her patience in reviewing all of the material contained in this book; her valuable suggestions, insights and critical review— and for reminding me of stories I had forgotten to include.

To my precious children, Tammy & Morris Rubin and Rabbi Uri & Shelli Karzen—who have given us so much Nachas, and who have always been an appreciative audience. Uri, my chief videographer at Bnai Mitzvah events, has been an eye witness to many of these, almost unbelievable but, true stories.

To my ten Sabra grandchildren— Elimelech, Odehya, Michael, Emunah, Elichai, Rachel, Neriyah, Nitzanit, Ben Zion and Avichayil— who, somehow cannot identify with the humor in this volume and do not find it terribly funny (yet)....

To Rabbi Reuven "Ruby" (Chaya Leah) Aberman— my Madrich (*Youth leader*) in Bnei Akiva and counselor at Camp Moshava during my teen years, and my mentor—who inspired me with a boundless love for Torah and Eretz Israel.

To: Rabbis Burton (Maxima) Wax and Benjamin (Simmie) Shandalov, lifelong cherished friends, who were my study companions (Chevruta) for years at the Hebrew Theological College of Chicago/Skokie and were my partners in the joy of Torah learning. They were a great influence in my formative years as we prepared for our rabbinic adventure.

To Sherwin and Shoni Pomerantz and Rabbi Oscar and Lillian Bookspan, special cherished friends, who offered sage advise and counsel in the organization of the material for this book and who lovingly urged and encouraged me to publish my anthology.

The disclaimer Poem, that follows, was inspired by Sherwin Pomerantz.

To: Rabbis Nachum Bronznick, Victor Bonchek, Macy Gordon, Hanoch Teller and Stewart Weiss for their technical assistance, insights and guidance regarding publication of my manuscript.

To a host of dear friends and neighbors, who have patiently listened to me relate these stories at their and our Shabbat table (and at choice restaurants) in Jerusalem:

Marvin & Barbara Silverman, Charles & Charlotte Gogek, Rabbi Abraham and Rachel Bruckenstein, Sid & Ruth Feibus, Rabbi Barry & Evelyn Bank, Rabbi Nathan & Leah Weiss, Herb & Toby Willig, Max & JennieWeil, Mordecai & Corinne Klar, Izzy & Edie Davidowitz, David & Norma Fund, Dr. Jeffrey & Myrna Buckman, Jeffrey & Zenia Cohen, Rabbi Barry (the late Judy) Rosen, Rabbi Douglas & Lois Zelden.

And our supportive, loving and caring Mishpacha (*family*) in the Diaspora: Rabbi Arthur & Judy Levin, Howard & Roslyn Zuckerman, Sandy & Linda Karzen. and Ilene (late Gary) Fierstien.

To Rebettzin Judy Blustein and her late husband, Rabbi-Chaplain Allan Marshall Blustein, lifelong family friends, who have always encouraged me to share my stories with the world.

Finally, Acharon, Acharon Chaviv— to the Almighty, who has given me the health and strength to serve in His Vineyard and allow me the opportunity to inspire and impact on our people with Ahavat Torah and Ahavat Yisrael. He has provided me with a keen sense of humor to be able to appreciate all of the many absurd moments in life and capture them for posterity.

Read and enjoy! And if you really enjoy, buy another copy and give it to a friend!

Jay Karzen

Chanukah 5759/1998 Our Bar Mitzvah Year of Aliyah

Preface

Rituals Unlimited

"And You Shall Hallow the Fiftieth Year" (Leviticus 25:10)

Rituals Unlimited was born on my 50th birthday when we made Aliyah (*"ascended" to Israel*) in December, 1985. Incidentally, we were now the first Karzen family in all of Jewish history (a) in the Jerusalem telephone book and (b) to pay taxes in two countries.

Realizing that thousands of youngsters come to Israel to celebrate their Bar/Bat Mitzvah and having officiated at well over thirteen hundred Bnai Mitzvah (plural for Bar/Bat Mitzvah) ceremonies in America, a career decision was made! Having been to Israel on numerous occasions and observing the "baalagon,"— haphazard, chaotic way— that Bar Mitzvah services are handled at the Western Wall, we felt that this could be my unique contribution to Israel. I would create a comprehensive service to upgrade the standards of the Bar Mitzvah experience at the Kotel (Wall)—and also at other popular venues like mount Masada, The Southern Wall Steps (south side of Temple Mount complex) and the roofless historic Hurva Synagogue in Jerusalem's Old City.

The Rituals Unlimited logo was chosen because of its unique all-inclusive connotation.

We would offer unlimited service to our tourist clientele. We boasted that our client families would have the best location at the Kotel and we would provide Hebrew/English prayer books, extra Talitot, (*prayer shawls*) Tefilin, (*phylacteries*) Kipot (*skullcaps*) and even supply the candy that is thrown at the celebrant following his Aliyah (*Torah honor*). We would offer professional videography and photography to capture this day for posterity and handle luncheon arrangements for the Seudat Mitzvah (*Feast*) following the Tefilah (*prayer service*). Any amenity to make this a worry-free experience for the family!

We expanded to also conduct Adult Bar/Bat Mitzvah celebrations, Weddings, Reaffirmation of Marriage Vows for couples coming here to celebrate special milestone anniversaries— Silver and/or Golden wedding Smachot. We have created every conceivable special life cycle ceremony —truly Rituals Unlimited!

During these dozen plus years we have handled countless Bar/Bat Mitzvah events and have incredibly funny stories and many humorous experiences to share. Read on and enjoy!

Website http://www.IsraelVisit.co.il.80/bar-mitzva/

A POETIC DISCLAIMER

As you stop to read this book,

Pause here first and give a look.

My intentions were to be airy and light,

But never a friend or acquaintance to slight.

I wanted to illustrate how humorous we are,

By sharing stories from near and far.

So relax, enjoy, take it as it was meant...

Even see it as a gift, heaven sent.

The Address of the Kotel

And so it begins..

A South African family was among the first to book me for their Bar Mitzvah celebration. In the process of printing invitations for their forthcoming event in Jerusalem, they faxed me with a simple question.

"What is the address of the Kotel?"

The service was to be at the Western Wall and the family wished to be precise and have the exact address on their official invitation. I assured them that no address was really necessary on the Bar Mitzvah invitation. The word Kotel or Western Wall was sufficient. Everyone knows where it is! No one would get lost and travel to Eilat or Haifa by mistake. No one would get "farblongett" (lost) and go to another Wall.

The family, however, was insistent. The next day another fax arrived and they persisted with the following question. "We realize that the Kotel is well known to everyone. Yet there must be an address. Everything has an address! Please find out the official address of the Western Wall and forward this to us ASAP?"

I called the various government authorities, from the City Hall to the Ministry of Religion. They all enjoyed a chuckle. If I were to have faxed the family that there is no address for the Kotel, they would not have believed me. So I composed an address. THE WESTERN WALL. ONE KOTEL PLAZA ! And believe me, that is exactly the way the invitation read.

So for your information: if you should ever be asked for the address of the holiest site in Jerusalem, copy the above in your address book. Someday, it may come in handy!

The Dancing Boys

One of the episodes that is indelibly etched in my memory is of the grandmother who brought her grandson to Jerusalem for his "2nd" Bar Mitzvah. The main service was in their home community in America and the celebrant's gift was a trip to Israel with Savta (grandmother) and a ceremony at the Kotel (Western Wall).

The night before the Simcha, I met the youngster and his grandmother. At this meeting we reviewed and rehearsed the service; and the youngster became comfortable with his "Rabbi for a Day!" This was an unusually small, intimate religious experience—and a meaningful bonding celebration for a grandmother and her grandson!

I asked the Savta if there were any special requests she had regarding the service.

"Yes", she proceeded to tell me, "I want the Kotel Dancing Boys to perform at our Bar Mitzvah!"

Dancing Boys?

I suggested that she was possibly confusing the fact that on

RABBI JAY'S WORLD OF HUMOR 23

Friday evenings at the Wall, the Yeshivat HaKotel (Rabbinical School near the Wall) student body comes down enmasse dancing and singing for the Kabbalat Shabbat (Friday night sunset) service. These are the famous "dancing boys" that all tourists look forward to seeing at the Kotel. Visitors often dance with them to celebrate the onset of Shabbat.

She insisted that her lady friend had also brought a grandson to Israel a year earlier for his Bar Mitzvah on a weekday morning and they had "dancing boys" at the service. She had seen the video of that service and wanted the same type of ceremony complete with the Jerusalem Kotel dancers for her grandson.

What was I to do?

My reputation was on the line. Our advertising boasts that we can arrange any amenity surrounding the Bar Mitzvah day. Where and how was I going to get dancing boys?

Needless to say, it was a sleepless night. We needed a miracle!

The family of two arrived on time. I gathered a Minyan for the Shachrit service. We began the prayers. Midway through the Tefillah, the Bubbe asked, from her side of the Mechitza, when the dancing boys are to arrive. I had hoped that she would forget, but she had not!

"Shortly," was my reply, hoping for some Nes (miracle).

And then it happened. . the miracle I had prayed for. A group of 30 youngsters from Raanana arrived at the Kotel as part of a class field trip. I approached the teacher of the class and implored him to help me by kindly asking his students to please do a "Mitzvah" —and save my reputation— All I needed was for them to dance and sing around our table for only a minute.

The educator was happy to assist me. The class came and sang for five minutes. We lifted the youngster on a chair during the Hakafot (circle) dancing (An extra point for me; Her friend's grandson was not lifted on a chair a year earlier). If you could have seen the joy on the face of this grandmother! I was a hero! I came through and got the dancing boys! And it was all recorded on the video cassette! How she kvelled (beamed with delight!)

There were dozens of other Bar Mitzvah services there that morning, but none of them, except mine, had dancing boys! To this day I can still vividly recall the beaming face of a proud grandmother.

I can visualize her boasting to her lady friends, how she found a Rabbi who supplies Dancing Boys and also lifts the youngster on a chair! She could have also boasted that she had a Dancing Rabbi. The truth is that I was so relieved that I was able to fulfill her request, that I danced also, as I've never danced before at a Bar Mitzvah. Rituals Unlimited did it again! Another satisfied client family.

To this day whenever I see a class field trip arrive at the Kotel, I am tempted to invite them to join us for a few moments, to add some Simcha to my service! There is nothing to compare to a Bar Mitzvah with Dancing Boys!

We Vote for No Tefilin

We handle Bar/Bat Mitzvah ceremonies for all denominations of Jews and each family is precious regardless of their Synagogue/Temple affiliation. Even the least observant families are amenable to experimenting with Tefilin, especially after I explain to them the significance and importance of this ritual artifact.

One family arrived for their Simcha and upon meeting with them, the mother announced that their family voted, on the flight overseas, not to use Tefilin for the Bar Mitzvah service at the Kotel! (As I learned subsequently, this family voted on almost everything. They were a very democratic Mishpacha! (family)

When I asked why they had voted against Tefilin, the answer I got was quite Talmudic—The "Kal V'Chomer" response.

(The Kal V'Chomer is one of the 13 Principles by which Judaism is interpreted. If for example a certain act is forbidden on an ordinary festival, it is so much the more forbidden on Yom Kippur. If an act is permissible on Yom Kippur, it is so much the more permitted on an ordinary festival).

This is how the family arrived at their decision to forego the Mitzvah of Tefilin.

The celebrants friends were understandably all having Bar Mitzvah services that season, all being thirteen years old. Some were conducted in Orthodox or Conservative Synagogues; others in Reform Temples. This family had been invited to two very Orthodox services on the SABBATH and noticed something very significant. None of the Orthodox Jews were wearing Tefilin on this most holy day of the week.

So, they reasoned, if religious Jews do not wear Tefilin on the holiest day of the week—The Sabbath— we, who are basically Reform Jews and not overly religious, should not have to wear the Tefilin on a mere weekday (The classic Kal V'chomer logic!)

On this basis the family voted unanimously on their El Al flight to celebrate the Bar Mitzvah, minus Tefilin. "But," the mother added, "we, also voted, that if the KNESSET requires Tefilin for a Kotel Bar Mitzvah, we will honor this law and abide by the decision of the Israeli government." Real Zionists!

I explained the significance and importance of the Tefilin and also why we do not wear this ritual item on Shabbat or major holidays. The family re-voted and were now most anxious to experiment with this "new" Mitzvah to which they had never before been exposed. Rituals Unlimited lends Tefilin to families who do not have their own or who refuse to buy them. I, jokingly, offer my Hertz Rent-a-Tefilin to my client families as part of my full package— at no additional charge.

After the Bar Mitzvah the family did VOTE to buy one pair of Tefilin to bring back to the States, to be shared by the male members of the family. But that is a wonderful beginning. Who knows how many times they have performed this holy mitzvah since their return from Israel?

If I had to vote, I would venture to opine that they have been occasionally used and in a few years when the next son is ready for his Bar Mitzvah, the family will proudly come back to Israel for the next Simcha with their religious equipment and they will vote to definitely use Tefilin again.

The Spooky Bar Mitzvah

A lovely family from the State of Utah arrived for a Bar Mitzvah. They were the only Jews in their community. There was no Synagogue/Temple within a radius of many miles, and consequently, they were not regular attendees at religious services. They were totally unfamiliar with Synagogue ritual.

The mother was most anxious to relate the "spooky" experience they had on the flight overseas. "Men gathered to pray with their Talit over their head. They were swaying back and forth. It was all so very spooky!"

An explanation was necessary. I offered an interpretation as to why Jews "sway when they pray." I suggested that perhaps Jews wished every part of their body to participate in the worship, not only the lips. This so impressed the family, that they inquired of me if at the Bar Mitzvah service the next morning I could recruit men for the minyan who would also sway.

I introduced into their limited Hebrew/Yiddish vocabulary, the expression: "shockel," which as any regular Shul attendee knows, is the act of aggressive swaying during the prayer service. They also requested that I invite men to join the minyan who would also place the Talit over their head. They obviously were moved by this practice. They had never before seen a Talit on the head, except one draped over the shoulders.

At the service the following morning, the Bar Mitzvah youngster was also getting into this newly discovered art of shockeling. He was having a great time imitating everyone around him.

The site of a swaying Jew at prayer with the Talit draped over the head, was no longer so spooky. The family told me after the completion of the Tefilah that they knew it would be nice, but didn't realize it would be so nice!

The Wrong Torah Portion

An American mixed-marriage family (the mother was Jewish) contacted us for a Thanksgiving Day Kotel Bar Mitzvah. In our first correspondence she proudly mentioned that her Israeli relatives were all Charedi (*ultra orthodox*)

Jews and would be in attendance.

To impress her religious family, she had hired a special teacher to prepare the youngster properly, so that he would be able to chant the Torah portion flawlessly.

Months of intensive study were spent by the celebrant in order to impress his religious relatives in Jerusalem. The teacher was a noted educator, the mother assured me, and the youngster even knew every "Shva Na and Shva Nach!" (technical grammatical pronunciations)

During my meeting with them the night before the service, I discovered that the celebrant had learned the wrong Torah portion. That Thursday (Thanksgiving Day in the USA) was also Rosh Chodesh, the new Hebrew month. There is a special monthly Torah reading on such days. How could the teacher in America have made such an obvious mistake? Rosh Chodesh is clearly marked on every Hebrew calendar.

What was I to do? Tell the family that the Rav hired to prepare the Bar Mitzvah celebrant had erred? How does one handle such a situation to avoid embarrassment and ruin what was to be a gala Simcha?

I told the family that there would be TWO Torah readings that day—the regular weekly portion that the Bar Mitzvah Bochur (lad) had learned so well and also a special reading in honor of the new Hebrew month. I called the Charedi patriarch of the family in Jerusalem and alerted him as to what was going to occur the next morning. I asked him to share my solution with the others who were going to be in attendance, and pleaded with him not to make an issue out of this delicate situation.

Let this be a real Simcha for the family and not even allude to the mistake made in preparing the youngster. After all, it wasn't the fault of the family.

There were two Torah readings! First we read the Rosh Chodesh portion and following that, the celebrant did his portion beautifully and flawlessly (with every Shva Na and Shva

Nach as promised.) The Bar Mitzvah family never did know about the wrong Parsha (portion) their son had been taught. The Orthodox congregants behaved with dignity and understanding and with a little flexibility, a potential disaster became a beautiful and memorable celebration.

Other Wrong Parsha Stories.

1) A family arrived for a scheduled Bar Mitzvah with a letter written in Hebrew from their Rabbi, sealed and addressed to me. The colleague wrote that this youngster is not a particularly talented student. He had memorized the Torah portion—the final verses (called Maftir)—for his first official Bar Mitzvah, which was held a few months earlier. He was now coming to Israel for a second ceremony.

It was not possible for this Bochur to learn ("memorize") another Torah portion. Therefore, he suggested that we open the Torah to the current weekly portion. I would read the appropriate Kriat HaTorah and then call the Bar Mitzvah and let him chant (by heart) the Maftir that he knew well. No one would know the difference!

2) During the pre-Bar Mitzvah meeting I discovered that instead of learning the opening verses of the weekly Torah portion, as it traditional for a Monday and Thursday, the celebrant had been prepared by his teacher to read the Maftir (closing portion) section.

The parents told me, when I questioned this unusual situation, that their Rabbi assured them that every Bar Mitzvah is expected to chant the Maftir—even in Israel! He supposedly also added that as long as you read something from the Torah, it makes no difference what is read.

3) On Mondays and Thursdays the Torah reading is generally the Shabbat first Aliyah portion subdivided into three smaller sections! A youngster once arrived from abroad having learned —amazingly—the entire first, second and third Shabbat aliyah, which amounted to almost half the entire Sedra. (Torah portion) His teacher insisted that in Israel we read three Full Aliyah segments during the weekdays and not only the first segmented aliyah as in the Diaspora. He had spent an entire year mastering the Kriah. I did not have the heart to tell him that his teacher erred. The youngster read, what was the longest Torah reading ever, on a regular Monday weekday morning.

4) The Torah portion following the Fast of Tisha B'av (commemorating destruction of both Temples) is always Vaetchanan. The highlight of this Sedra is the Ten Commandments. A youngster came prepared to read these Aseret HaDibrot (10 Commandments) for his Bar Mitzvah. Unfortunately, this selection doesn't appear until much later into the Sedra.

It seems that in his Congregation, each candidate for Bar Mitzvah can choose his favorite verses of the weekly portion and then, that becomes the Torah reading for his service. His Rabbi explained that it is not necessary to always read the first verses.

As long as something significant is read from the weekly portion, it is a Kosher (proper) Kriat Hatorah. (Torah reading)

The "God Loves Humming" Bar Mitzvah

Each celebrant has his own unique personality. They are darling youngsters and each supplies his family with an abundance of Nachas during the Bar Mitzvah service. We make sure of that!

During the rehearsal meeting, I asked a youngster what prayers he might be able to chant besides the Torah blessings and the short Torah reading he had prepared.

"Well," he said, "I attend Religious school and know most of the prayers."

Thrilled that he was so anxious to do more than the average celebrant, I asked the obvious. "How about Adon Olom (Master of the World)? You know that there are dozens and dozens of different melodies to this important prayer. Which is your favorite?"

"I know them all," he replied, and began to HUM one melody after the other

"What about the words?" I inquired.

"I'm not so good with the words but I know all the melodies!" was his response.

He began to HUM every prayer I suggested, from Baruch Sheamar to Ashray; from Alenu to Ayn Kaylokaynu (all of above are names of important popular morning service prayers.) He knew all the basic traditional chants but not one word of the prayers.

The parents and grandparents were most impressed that their Bar Mitzvah Bochur (youngster) had such talents. So he didn't know the words—big deal! But he knew the melodies and chants. He could HUM all the prayers!

Not missing the opportunity to reassure the family, a new concept was created: GOD LOVES HUMMING!

I explained to the assembled guests that humming with tremendous Kavanna (concentration and devotion) was more precious to God's ears than mere prayers recited routinely without sincere devotion.

Our Bar Mitzvah celebrant was going to demonstrate true devotion through his ability to hum the prayers, and this was going to pierce the very gates of heaven. The videographers and photographers never know what to expect from Rituals Unlimited's creative Bar Mitzvah services.

We dovened (prayed) Shachrit (morning service) and we hummed our way through much of it. It was a Bar Mitzvah to remember. It certainly was a different, unique service! There were many simultaneous Bnai Mitzvah services being recited at the Kotel. I suspect that Hashem (the "Name" denoting the Almighty) looking down and listening to all of the Tefilot that morning, somehow, got a lot of pleasure at our humming Shachrit. He couldn't have missed this special, atypical, but very genuine, worship.

The "Start Me Off" Bar Mitzvah

One celebrant came totally unprepared for his Bar Mitzvah. He hadn't learned the Torah portion nor any other section of the liturgy. It seems that the travel agent assured the family that when they arrived in Israel and met with the Rabbi, he would supply all that the youngster needed to recite for the ceremony.

While it is true that occasionally I do have to supply the transliterated Torah blessings and other major prayers for those students who do not attend religious school, this youngster attended Hebrew School and it was puzzling that he had come totally unaware of what was expected of him.

"Do you know some of the basic popular prayers?" I innocently inquired.

"Sure, I know almost all of the main prayers," he boasted.

Relieved, I asked, him if he knew the most important of the prayers, The Shma Yisrael.

"Of course," was his reply.

"Wonderful, could you please sing it for me?"

His response startled me.

"Start Me Off!"

There are only six words to this prayer, so I chanted in the traditional melody, the first two words."Yes, I know that," the celebrant continued. "Sing a few more of the words, please!"

And so, there I was singing the entire verse for him. He didn't know the Shma Yisrael even after I had started him off.

We continued to the other prayers and whatever Tefilah I suggested—be it Adon Olom, Ashray, Amidah—he proudly announced that he knew all of these prayers— if I could only start him off!

I suggested that he might lead us in these basic prayers during the service, rather than recite them in solo. Actually we would chant them in duet. I would start and he would then join with me. And that is how "Mister Start Me Off" celebrated his Bar Mitzvah.

The videographer, fully briefed, focused on him and came in for close-ups after I had started off each prayer. Another Rituals Unlimited Bar Mitzvah to long remember!

The Baseball Bat Bat Mitzvah

One afternoon I received a telephone call from a family inquiring if I was the famous Bar Mitzvah King, a nickname given to me in a feature article that appeared in the local Jerusalem Post. A grandfather had come to Israel from New York with two teenage granddaughters for a belated double Bat Mitzvah. They wanted to meet and interview me to see if I was the proper Rabbi for their Simcha.

In preparation for our meeting, I even brought along a copy of my Semicha, in case they wished to see proof of my ordination. This was my first "interview" with a prospective client family. No one had ever questioned my qualifications before!

I met the lovely young girls and the grandfather. The spokesman handling the interview was another family member — a cousin of the girls. I am not sure exactly why he was even there or how he became involved in this entire episode. I was not asked any Halachic questions or anything regarding my religious qualifications or knowledge of Bat Mitzvah ceremonies. Nor did anyone ask to see my Semicha (ordination diploma).

"Rabbi," the cousin proudly said, "We are all avid baseball fans and we are looking for a Rabbi to handle the Bnot Mitzvah (plural for Bat Mitzvah) who shares our enthusiasm for this sport!"

I quickly responded that I am, indeed, a major baseball fan and my favorite team is the Chicago Cubs. Coincidentally, the Cubs were also the teenagers favorite team.

I'm still not sure why anyone NOT from Chicago would be a Cubs baseball fan.

"Are you willing to answer some baseball questions so we can be absolutely sure that you are a rabbinical baseball authority?" continued the relative. The pressure mounts!

Never in my life did I ever expect that my being engaged to conduct a Bar/Bat Mitzvah would hinge on my knowledge of baseball statistics.

Rather than be exposed to some offbeat questions or obscure facts that I could not be expected to know, I began to volunteer the following information.

The last time the Chicago Cubs won the National League pennant and played in the World Series was 1945. I proceeded to list the batting order of that years championship team. I related to them the batting averages of the stars of the team and even the numbers on their uniforms. I also related some trivia about being present when one of the players hit his only major league home run. I spoke for 10 minutes about the '45 Cubs team. They were so impressed with my vast knowledge of this team, who had not won another title in over fifty years, that the spokesman-cousin turned to the grandfather and girls and announced: "This is our Rabbi!"

I was engaged to conduct a brief, mostly English ceremony at the historic outdoor Hurva Synagogue. I created a special service for these teenage baseball fans, who had a maximum know-

-ledge of baseball but a very minimal knowledge of Judaism. The plan was to have a closing segment of the Bat Mitzvah in the Kotel Plaza after the Hurva service.

The story is not over yet...

The double Bat Mitzvah was very moving. We read Psalms about Jerusalem. The girls read English readings that I composed specifically for this occasion. We added special prayers relevant to this Simcha and they each delivered a brief speech. Each celebrant received a gift of a challah cover and an impressive certificate from the Ministry of Tourism.

Now it was time to make our way down to the Kotel Plaza. As we walked together, making our way through the Jewish Quarter to the Western Wall Plaza, both the grandfather and the cousin were passing out dollar bills to all the children playing in the "Rova" area. As we approached a snack shoppe, leading down to the Kotel, they, Pied Piper-like, gathered the dozens of children ordering ice-cream and drinks for each one. I estimated that between the dollar bills they generously distributed and the snacks he had purchased, he had spent close to $100.

Following the closing ceremony near the Kotel, the service having been completed, it was now time to settle the rabbinic honorarium. The cousin apologetically explained that they could not possibly pay the sum printed on the official price list, because "it's very costly to hang around the Kotel area. There are so many unforeseen expenses." He, then handed me a token fee and promised the balance when he returned home.

I never expected to see them again or receive any additional check!

That night, my wife and I were out with friends at a local restaurant — and who should be sitting there — but this family— When they realized I was present they sent over a bottle of complimentary wine for our table "In Honor of THEIR Rabbi." Now for sure, I thought, I'd never get the balance , since the wine was very expensive.

A month later, the check did arrive with an added bonus! A note of appreciation was attached, thanking me for the inspirational service and for exposing them to the beauty of our religion. One of the young girls even mentioned that she hoped to return to Israel and possibly go to college in Jerusalem! The other wrote that she hoped to make Aliyah some day!

P.S. I should mention that my sermonette to the celebrants naturally was a baseball theme. As their Rabbi "manager," I reminded them, as they now stepped into the batter's box, never to forget to touch all of life's bases; never to stop short and always remember that to score in life, you have to touch home base! The Synagogue is our home base. I alluded to the fact that sometimes on the path of life we strikeout; sometimes we commit errors; some even walk outside the baseline; some folks are always balking and some speak foul language. I used every bit of the baseball terminology in my remarks. But I did get through to the celebrants! They will never forget this experience and neither will I!

The CD-ROM Bar Mitzvah.

A family, who were very much into computers, communicated that their son was to be one of the first youngsters to learn his Torah portion from a CD-Rom. They had arranged for the preparation of their son's Bar Mitzvah material via this newest medium.

At the rehearsal meeting the proud celebrant chanted the verses from the Torah portion of Tazria with the following endings:

Vydaber Hashem el Mosheh Laymorrrrrrrrrrrrrrrrrrr.
. . El Hakohennnnnnnnnnnn
. . Min Hatzaruaaaaaaaaaaaaaaaa
. . V'ayzovvvvvvvvvvvvvvv
. . El Mayim Chayimmmmmmmm.
  A unique style! Different, interesting, distinctive!
  The parents were beaming and awaiting my approval.
  At the Kotel the next morning, the several dozen worshippers stood stunned as they listened to this unusual interpretation. Some stared in the air as if to ask themselves if they were hearing correctly. Was something wrong with their ears? Others looked this way and that to make eye contact with the next person and ask "Are you hearing the same as I am"? Some of the youngsters started to giggle.
  A CD-Rom success story? I'm not so sure!

The Priest and the Tefilin

Standing in my corner, near the Mechitza, (fence separating the men and women) waiting for a Bar Mitzvah family to arrive, there are always questions to answer from the throngs of tourists. They range from the reason for the Talit and Tefilin to why the Bar Mitzvah is held on Mondays and Thursdays to why the need to separate the sexes during prayer; and why some of the men wear funny black clothing, etc.

One morning a group of Catholics from Italy surrounded me and inquired about what Jews believe regarding heaven and hell, the Messiah and Reward and Punishment. I enjoyed sharing with them some basic Judaic information.

The Priest, who was the leader of the group, suddenly turned to me and asked if it would be permissible for him to don the Tefilin. He had always felt a need to do so and seeing the half dozen sets of Tefilin on the Shulchan, (table) awaiting the Bar Mitzvah family, he wished my permission to have the privilege of placing the Tefilln on his arm and head for a few moments.

My first thought was "Halavai, (if only) every Jew would wish that same privilege!"

How many Jewish guests at Bar Mitzvah refuse to perform this Mitzvah and find every conceivable excuse not to do so. Here is a non-Jew who craves the honor of having these black boxes on his person.

I allowed him to be photographed with the Tefilin as I wrapped them on his hand and head. Not all of the Chassidim (black garbed pious Jews), witnessing this phenomenon, necessarily approved of my liberal approach to this matter. But the priest, to my surprise, wearing the Tefilin suddenly shouted out in perfect Hebrew "SHMA YISRAEL." (Hear, O Israel)

I have a gut feeling that this clergyman could have been a Jew by birth and somewhere along the line got sidetracked. If this is so, I helped a lost Jew perform a Mitzvah. If he was not a born Jew, at least I allowed a "colleague" to fulfill his fantasy and possibly also performed a Kiddush Hashem (Sanctification of the Name) for the sake of brotherhood.

I am sure that the picture of this priest wearing Tefilin hangs proudly in his church, somewhere in Italy. Sometimes you do an impetuous act and are not sure if it was the right thing to do or not! In this specific instance, I have never regretted doing what I did and would do it again.

(This priest may someday be the next Pope. Who is that Rabbi in the picture with the Pope?)

The Bread & Wine Bar Mitzvah

Each youngster comes to his Bar Mitzvah with specific ritual talents and abilities. Some prepare to read from the Torah and others are able to chant the liturgy and serve as the Cantor. A few come with minimal background and can only chant the two Torah Blessings.

One youngster proudly announced that he had only been able to master the two main blessings. That was all he was prepared to do for his service. I assumed he was referring to the traditional Torah Blessings (the one recited before and the second after the Torah Reading.) But he meant something else.

He had come to Israel having learned the Blessing for Bread (Hamotzi Lechem Min HaAretz) and the Blessing for Wine. (Boray Pree Hagaffen) How do you build a Bar Mitzvah service around those two popular, but inappropriate blessings? Don't ask how and what we did, but suffice it to say this youngster had a Kosher Bar Mitzvah!

The All in Hebrew Bar Mitzvah

A celebrant insisted, at our pre-Bar Mitzvah rehearsal meeting, that I speak and conduct the service in Ivrit (Hebrew)—no English at all.

When I questioned the youngster as to his fluency in Hebrew, he unashamedly boasted that he understood very little of the language but since this is Israel and that Hebrew is the official language of the country, he wished to have his Bar Mitzvah conducted exclusively in that language.

"But you won't understand anything," I retorted, "and this is my big opportunity to share our beautiful religion with you. If I speak in Hebrew, you will not understand one word." The family agreed with their son. If this is what he wanted, the Rabbi has to accede to his wishes.

The service began and whatever was explained to him was not grasped—whether Tefillin, Siddur or prayers. He remained glassy-eyed and uncomprehending.

Finally, in desperation and frustration, I asked permission of the family to offer some English words. They were grateful that they would finally understand the beauty of what was transpiring. I suspect that the Bar Mitzvah Bochur was glad that I had made a unilateral decision to stop this farce and begin speaking in a comprehensible language. From that point on the service became meaningful. The youngster was relieved. He could now understand what was happening on this big day in his life!

Another Rituals Unlimited special Bar Mitzvah to long remember!

Rosh Chodesh (The New Month)

I received a midnight call from Canada, inquiring whether they might change an already confirmed date to a few days earlier. When I inquired as to why they wished the change, they replied that they were told by friends that a Rosh Chodesh (new month) service was a very lovely service, and consequently, they wishes the change. They wanted a lovelier service!

While it was not a technical problem for me to alter my calendar, I asked the caller if she knew that the service was significantly longer with the addition of the Hallel (psalms of praise) and Musaf (the additional prayers added on special days.)

"Rabbi, please do not make it too long. We don't want a boring service. We want the lovely Rosh Chodesh service!"

"Do you know what Rosh Chodesh is?" I continued. She hadn't a clue.

We were only a few weeks away from the Simcha and I assumed that the youngster had already been prepared with the Torah portion for that week. When I informed the woman that if we changed the date, there was a special and different Torah reading. Would her son be able to master a new Kriah, having already invested a year of study on the portion of the week?

"Oh no! That would be out of the question. He has already memorized the Torah section.

Is that a major problem to have him read what he has learned? What's the difference what is read, as long as he reads something?"

P.S. The date was changed. We read both the weekly and the Rosh Chodesh reading.

He did the former and I the latter. We sang the Hallel, we recited Musaf and the family was happy to have had a lovely Rosh Chodesh service. It took a bit longer, by necessity, but nobody seemed to mind. It was a lovely service!

Don't Make it Tight

A family pleaded with me not to tie the Tefilin too tightly on their son's hand during the Bar Mitzvah. They had heard "horror" stories of how some Rabbis insist on wrapping the straps so tightly that it becomes an unpleasant religious experience.

Promising the anxious mother and father that I would wrap the straps as loosely as possible, the youngster also kept reminding me to remember my pledge. "Don't make it tight!"

As the service began, the straps began to unwind and slip down the celebrants left hand. And so did his new large Talit fall off his shoulders. As inconspicuously as possible, I began to re-tie and re-wind the straps and adjust his Talit, without trying to attract too much attention. It happened once and it happened twice; and it occurred a third and fourth time. All during the Tefilah I was fixing his Tefilin and rearranging his prayer-shawl. Everyone was now witnessing this phenomenon; it was impossible not to notice.

Instead of concentrating on the service, it became a situation of how long will the straps remain in place without them (and the Talit) slipping down again. Finally, in desperation, I tightened the straps properly to insure that they wouldn't again slide down the arm. Now they were reasonably tight. I held my hand on his shoulder so that the Talit would not slide down again.

Following the service, as we were removing the Tefilin, the youngster said to me: "Rabbi, if you would have tied them more securely on my hand in the first place, they wouldn't have slipped down so often."

You can't always win!

Peaking Too Soon

Every youngster is a superstar on his Bar Mitzvah day! Each celebrant brings much Nachas (pride) to his family as he chants his Torah portion. Occasionally, there is an exception to this rule.

A nervous lad had made mistake after mistake during the Torah service. He even erred in the chanting of the simple Torah blessings. This poor chap mispronounced every other word and seemed relieved when he actually read a word correctly. It was obvious to all the assembled guests that he had minimum ritual skills.

What can a Rabbi say—and what should he say—following such a performance?

Before I had a chance to say a word, the embarrassed mother, from across the Mechitza (separation fence) was heard to say: "My son peaked at age 10 and I guess it's been downhill ever since!"

Good, Better, Best !

Often I will ask the Bar/Bat Mitzvah, before I present the official Ministry of Tourism certificate, to promise me never to say to anyone: "I am a good Jew." After his initial shock, I continue to explain thusly.

On the ladder of superlatives there is GOOD, BETTER and BEST. Good is the lowest level and there is no reason to be proud of being on the bottom of the ladder. You may say: "I WAS a good Jew; now I am a better Jew and someday I hope to reach my Jewish best."

Once I was in the midst of this thought, listing the three rungs of the ladder — good, better, best. I asked the celebrant: "Of these three words — good, better, best — which is the LOWEST rung?"

To help the youngster, I dramatically gestured at each word. For "good" I lowered my hand. For "better" I held my hand straight and for "best" I lifted my hand high in the air. I repeated this exercise twice. "Now", I asked, "which is the lowest rung?"

The mother shouted out to her son, from across the Mechitza fence: "Say Best!"

The father, also pre-empting the celebrant, said:" No! say Better!"

The audience of tourists, listening in disbelief from the Kotel Plaza, all yelled out in unison to the Bar Mitzvah:

"Say GOOD!"

There were only three possibilities and now the youngster was totally confused.

I whispered the answer to him and, amazingly, he got it right!

The Sentimental Tattered Talit

There were families who proudly displayed a grandfather's (or great grandfather's) old tattered and torn Talit. For sentimental reasons they wished their son to don this prayer garment for the service at the Kotel. My response depended on my mood. If I were anxious for a confrontation, I would ask if they would also allow their son to wear an old suit or shirt that was left by the deceased. They obviously would not agree to their child wearing such old clothing.

Why was a Talit different? I once told a family that if this prayer shawl was so sentimental, they should frame it and hang it on their wall, but not let their son wear it during services! They were introduced to the concept of " Zeh Kayli V'anvehu"-This is my God and I will glorify Him (Exodus 15:2)— which requires us to perform Mitzvot with the most beautiful ritual garb, not necessarily the oldest.

What Happened to the Tzitzit?

During a pre-Bar Mitzvah meeting with the family at their hotel, the proud parents displayed their son's new Talit (prayer shawl)—a gift from the grandparents. The mother had trimmed off the lengthy Tzitzit (required specially knotted strings on all four corners) from the new Talit. She wished her son's Talit to be neat!

Staring at this truncated garment in amazement, I suspect she thought that the lengths of string, hanging from the knots, were expendable. I have never seen such a strange looking Talit!

Forgetting the Melody

An inquiry: Is it permissible according to Jewish law for a father to teach his own son the Torah portion for the Bar Mitzvah?

After assuring the caller that it was indeed permitted—even according to the most strict rabbinic authorities—he was a bit embarrassed to confess that he had forgotten the melody for the Torah reading.

"Rabbi, I don't attend the Synagogue too often. Unfortunately, I have forgotten the melody for the Torah reading. Could you please send me a cassette tape with the correct melody so I can begin preparing my son?"

I tried to explain that the Torah reading is more than a simple melody. There are cantillations, called Trop, over or under each word. These Trop are the musical notes that make up the melody. But he assured me that if I could tape the basic melody, his son, who is very musical, could figure out the way to make the Torah reading very melodious.

The family received more than the melody. I recorded the

entire reading. At the Bar Mitzvah, the father was praised as being a master teacher!

And What's Inside the Tefilin?

Occasionally, I ask questions of the youngsters on the eve of their Bar Mitzvah.

Sometimes I will ask what the words "Bar Mitzvah" mean; other times I will ask if the celebrant can name the Patriarchs and the Matriarchs or the Five Books of Moses. I might ask them to list some of the Ten Commandments.

During one month, I decided to ask each youngster if they knew what was inside the Tefilin. These are some of the answers I got.

> The Ten Commandments
> The Book of Esther
> The Five Books of Moses
> The 23rd Psalm
> The 613 Commandments
> The Adon Olom prayer
> Kol Nidre (Yom Kippur prayer)
> HaTikvah (The Israeli National Anthem)
> A Mezuza
> The important commandments
> The warranty
> Nothing at all!

(Very few could correctly answer that there are four selected chapters of the Torah inside the Tefilin with the "Shma Yisrael" being one of the passages).

A colleague once asked his students to name the Ten Commandments in any order.

A clever student responded: 2-4-8-10-1-3-5-7-6-9.

Teen Usherettes

A wealthy South American family wished to guarantee that the dozens of women expected for their Kotel Bar Mitzvah service would be able to see, hear and be close enough to the actual Tefilah (prayer service). They wanted an entire area cordoned off near the Mechitza fence.

We engaged teen usherettes, who arrived at sunrise and by stationing themselves every few feet near the desired area, blocked off prime women's standing space near the prestigious Kotel Karzen Korner. When the group arrived, each woman had an ideal spot from which to witness and participate fully in the Simcha.

Needless to mention, other families who were also there to celebrate a Bar Mitzvah were not too happy with these young, aggressive usherettes, who physically limited access to the women's area.

Remember the anonymous maxim: "All is fair in love and war?"

The author forgot to also include: "and vying for a prime place at the Kotel!"

The Woman Rabbi and the Talit

During services for non-traditional families, we often have explanatory segments throughout the service. The Tefilah thus becomes also an educational lesson. For example, as we approach the Shma Yisrael prayer, the worshippers are requested to gather together the Tzitzit fringes from the four corners of their Talitot. I proceed to explain the significance of the fringes and why it is a beautiful custom to kiss these strings.

Once, in the course of the explanation, a woman, from alongside the Mechitza, interrupted to ask if this tradition applies to a woman wearing a Talit. I had never before had a female wear this prayer garment. Nor had I noticed her praying with us with a large kosher Talit draped over her shoulders.

I did a double-take. I was so surprised by both her question and by seeing her at the Kotel in a Talit, that my head moved from looking straight ahead and then at this Talit-clad young lady. The video captured this "double take" for posterity.

After the service concluded and we had a chance to speak, I discovered that she was a Rabbi from the States and had decided to pray with my group wearing a Talit. I never asked why she opted not to wear Tefilin!

All of a Sudden

Often we will get requests to recite the traditional Memorial Prayer (El Malay Rachamim) at the Bar Mitzvah, following the Torah service, for deceased grandparents or other family members who have gone to their eternal reward.

One family had a lengthy list of people they wished me to include during this solemn remembrance. As the father of the Bar Mitzvah read me the names, he added "All of a Sudden" following each deceased loved one. I assumed he wished to inform me that they had died suddenly or prematurely.

But then I realized, what he meant to say was "ALAV HASHALOM". (May he rest in peace) He knew that it was traditional to always add, following the name of a deceased individual, the tribute "Alav Hashalom." But as a youngster, when he heard others do so, it registered to his ears, not as Alav Hashalom, but rather as All of A Sudden.

The Mashiach in the Kitchen

We had booked a Bar Mitzvah and had also arranged for a post service party (Seudat Mitzvah) at one of the prestigious kosher restaurants. A few weeks before the Simcha, a humorous fax arrived from the family informing me that they were expecting many religious guests at their event.

The anxious mother, possibly fearful that some of the ultra orthodox family/friends might not eat at their simcha, requested that I call the proprietor of the restaurant and have him guarantee that the MASHIACH would be in the kitchen throughout the party to certify the highest Kashrut (Kosher) standards.

A Mashgiach is a dietary law supervisor. The Mashiach is the Messiah and not personally involved with Kashrut. It is easy to confuse the two words.

I called the manager and told him of the request. After the predictable laughter and humorous question: "Do they want to see his white donkey in our parking lot?" He arranged for the Mashgiach to be visible all afternoon.

Everyone ate heartily!

All through the meal, though, I couldn't help but look toward the kitchen to be certain as to who was actually there!

On What Day Will The Messiah Arrive?

Based on the Talmudic discussion in Tractate Eruvin (43 a/b) as to when the Messiah will arrive, I have a recurring nightmare that he might come on an early Monday or Thursday.

As everyone certainly knows, Bar Mitzvah services are scheduled at the Kotel on these two mornings!

Can you imagine the "baalagon"--the confusion and utter chaos-around the Old City of Jerusalem, should the Mashiach (Messiah) arrive on Bar Mitzvah day? Traffic is already highly congested on these busy mornings. It is already difficult to drive in the vicinity of the Kotel on these two days.

With the media covering this historic event and with the throngs of people converging on Jerusalem to welcome the long awaited for Savior---my Bar Mitzvah families will certainly come late for their service. Traffic will be at a virtual standstill. Even taxicabs won't be allowed in the area. And if it should be one of my very busy days with multiple Bar Mitzvah events, it will throw off the entire schedule.

So, while I am a devout believer in the coming of the Mashiach. and truly believe that he can come at any time, I pray that it will occur on a SUNDAY, TUESDAY, WEDNESDAY OR FRIDAY!

But please, never on a Monday or Thursday.

Praying To Phyllis

Are Jews supposed to be superstitious? Absolutely not! Non-Jews often have statues of saints in their automobiles as good luck charms.

I was once asked by a guest, before a Bar Mitzvah began:

"If we are, indeed, a non-superstitious people, why do observant Jews offer a prayer to a saint called Phyllis each time they drive outside the city limits?"

A bit shocked, I could not fathom his question. What religious Jew prays to a Phyllis? Saint Phyllis? What kind of nonsense?

Then I realized that he was referring to the popular "traveler's prayer" known in Hebrew as TEFILAS HADERECH. (Sephardic pronunciation: Tefilat HaDerech)

Tefilas.. sounded to his ears as To Phyllis!

The Movie and the CNN Crew

Again, in my Karzen Korner, awaiting the arrival of my first Bar Mitzvah family of the day, a movie crew, complete with professional actors, a director and cameramen began preparations for filming a tourism promotional —featuring a Bar Mitzvah at the Kotel.

The director was obviously unhappy with the "Rabbi-actor" sent by the casting office.

He didn't feel that a pony tail and earrings fit the image for an officiating Rabbi. They asked me if I was willing to assist them in their film. I would be the rabbinic star in the movie!

It seems that the production staff had also forgotten to bring along a Talit and Tefilin and the other necessary items. My ritual equipment was used in the film and the crew appreciated my willingness to cooperate. I also offered technical assistance in guiding them as to what to highlight in preparing this important documentary to promote (Bar Mitzvah) tourism to Israel.

Among other places, this clip is shown on most El Al flights around the world.

That same month, a CNN crew came to the Kotel to film a segment for their popular "Sights and Sounds" segment on Israel. They spent an hour scouting the Kotel for an ideal Bar Mitzvah scene to capture for posterity. They opted to feature me wrapping Tefilin on a youngster's arm and reciting the blessing with him.

This commercial for Israel is viewed all over the world.

All in a day's work at the Western Wall!

VIPs at Bar Mitzvah

Over the years, Rituals Unlimited has hosted the Chief Rabbi of Israel, cabinet ministers and members of the Knesset, who have come to participate in Bnai Mitzvah celebrations.

One early summer morning, standing at the Kotel Karzen Korner, a contingent of security personnel approached, in preparation for the arrival of the United States Ambassador to our country, Martin Indyk. The prestigious guest was scheduled to attend the Bar Mitzvah of the son of a close friend.

They knew my name and were most pleased at the prime location arranged for the service.

They proceeded to "secure" the corner. By the time the family and distinguished guest arrived, a large crowd had gathered to see who the VIP was to be.

Imagine the delight of the primarily Orthodox spectators as they witnessed Mr. Indyk perform the Mitzvah of Talit/Tefilin and have an Aliyah L'Torah (Torah honor) and even dance with the Bar Mitzvah celebrant. He even assisted in lifting the celebrant on a chair for the traditional Mitzvah dance.

Here was one youngster who will never forget his Bar Mitzvah ceremony!

The No-Show Bar Mitzvah

What was our most unforgettable Bar Mitzvah? The one where the youngster failed to show. The four grandparents, aunts, uncles, cousins and friends were there. Close to fifty people were in attendance at 8 AM, waiting for the appearance of the Bar Mitzvah and his parents. They never arrived.

The family lived in Raanana and were to drive to the Kotel that morning. The rest of the guests were Jerusalemites or tourists staying in local hotels.

That morning a massive demonstration by the Aviation Industry, protesting the cancellation of the Lavi aircraft contract, closed all the roads to Jerusalem from the airport junction. The family was caught in this closure and unable to proceed. By 9 AM we heard the news and assumed that the family would not be able to arrive.

So we prayed without the Bar Mitzvah and his parents! Members of the family shared the honors of being Baalay Tefilah, (cantors) both grandfathers had Aliyot and I gave a blessing to the absentee celebrant. We sang and danced and it was a wonderful Simcha—even without the Baal Simcha.

This Bar Mitzvah will always be remembered because it was the only service we ever did without the Bar Mitzvah celebrant present.

The "Conservative" Talit?

A family, consisting of father/mother, Bar Mitzvah celebrant and one set of proud grandparents arrived for the Simcha. The Saba (grandfather)intercepted me before my hotel meeting and asked if I had time the next day to accompany him and the young lad to the Meah Shearim neighborhood so that he could buy his grandson a Talit. He wished me to assist and advise him on the correct type of prayer shawl to purchase.

In the car the grandfather began lecturing the young man on the importance of tradition. He boasted of being a proud and faithful "Conservative" Jew and wanted his grandson to follow in his example as a proud Conservative Jew, and purchase a Conservative Talit. I interrupted and asked what exactly he meant by a Conservative Talit The response was as I expected it to be.

"A Talit that fits over the shoulders like a scarf. Not the big Orthodox ones that hang draped over the shoulders!"

I tactfully suggested that the scarf Talitot are not exactly 100% Kosher since a Talit must cover at least half the body and the scarf style prayer shawls don't meet that religious requirement. I also told him that most of my Bnai Mitzvah youngsters were opting for the bigger style Talit and many of them were even Reform Jews.

But he insisted that he wanted his grandson to wear the same type of Talit that he and his father had worn a generation ago. "We want to preserve the Conservative tradition in our family!" he stubbornly argued.

We entered one of the many religious supply stores in this ultra orthodox area and the grandfather requested from the proprietor to show him a variety of Conservative Talitot (he used the Yiddish word: Taleisim). The elderly salesman looked at me and I shrugged my shoulders. I doubt if he ever heard that term before (Conservative Talit?) But he did have a large variety of black, blue, maroon scarf Talitot and the youngster tried each of them on for size but didn't seem to like any that were shown him. Suddenly the thirteen year old noticed the big Talitot and asked to try them on for size. The grandfather grew pale. "No, No, these are not for us. We must perpetuate the Conservative tradition and wear a smaller scarf Talit."

The celebrant was stubbornly attracted to the larger versions. First he tried on a black and white Talit and then a blue and white Talit. He couldn't make up his mind which he liked best. He jokingly suggested maybe to buy both so he could alternate between the two. Now the grandfather was angry at both his grandson and me. I wasn't being much of a help. He assumed I would urge the celebrant to listen to his grandfather.

Grandpa had lost. The youngster absolutely would not even consider a small Talit. He wanted a big man's Kosher Orthodox Talit. The grandfather was forced to purchase this gift against his will and with a tear in his eyes.

At the formal ceremony of donning the Talit as we commenced the Bar Mitzvah service, I didn't know if I should mention to the group that it was a gift from the proud grandfather, but I did do so! All the guests commented on the magnificent new Talit being worn by the celebrant, but throughout the service I could feel the resentment towards me by the "Conservative" Zayda.

Months later, I learned, that shortly after their return to America the grandfather suddenly died. I only hope that deep in his heart he realized that he had done the right thing and had purchased for his only grandson a truly Kosher Talit. More importantly I hope he realized that there is no such thing as a Conservative Talit!

The Partner

Everyone is in awe of the Kotel. Despite the crowds, the pushing, the "baalagon" and often uncomfortable position for the women, who wish to get closer, see and fully participate in their son's Bar Mitzvah— there is electricity at the Kotel that makes a celebration there a truly wonderful religious experience.

(A family once arrived for an end of December Simcha, and arrived early enough to be able to include a trip to Bethlehem on December 24 — to have another religious experience!)

The only major complaint of my client families, are the beggars, who seem to outnumber, at times, the worshippers. At the entrance and exit, the charity collectors swarm about each person approaching the Wall. And they can easily recognize the tourist. Often, they also interrupt the service at the most awkward times and request Tzadakah. (charity donations)

A service had just concluded and the father was signing travelers checks at the Shulchan table, where we had just celebrated a very wonderful, joyous Simcha. As the checks for the videographer and photographer were being signed, a beggar lady—one of the regulars at the Wall, to whom I usually give a shekel—looked over the Mechitza, saw the amounts of the checks, and began to berate me:

"You get so much money and you only give me a shekel?"

I was stunned by her loud rebuke.

"Are you now my partner?" I questioned in disbelief at her effrontery.

"If so, do you want to share in my business expenses also? There is advertising, printing, mailings, faxes, long distance calls, E-mail and so much more!"

Muttering to herself, she stalked away and that was the shortest partnership in history!

The Cellphone: A Call From on High..

At a recent Bar Mitzvah on the awesome heights of Masada—deep in the Judean Desert—the inevitable occurred! During a very dramatic point in the ceremony, the shrill sound of a ringing cellphone interrupted the solemnity of the moment.

As you might guess, the single Israeli, amidst the Congregation of tourists, was receiving a personal telephone call from a friend.

That's life in one of the oldest/newest sites on earth. Modern Israel!

Tear Gas at The Kotel

One Purim eve (holiday commemorating the deliverance of the Jews from a massacre in 450 BCE) on the Fast of Esther (heroine of the holiday), I arrived early to secure my favorite corner alongside the Mechitza. A group of women came into the Ezrat Nashim (women's prayer area) that morning with the intent of conducting their own service. A few dozen ladies, some with Talitot, began to quietly chant the Shachrit service.

Their presence attracted an angry reaction from some of the female regulars who daily pray at the Kotel. Their shouts attracted some of the male ultra Orthodox worshippers.

Within seconds a semi-riot broke out with men hurling heavy chairs over the Mechitza fence at the women. The police were called in and only restored order after they fired tear gas to disperse the rioters.

I was standing in the back right corner protecting my small area for my family due to arrive in a half hour. Never having been in a tear gas attack before, I assumed that merely by covering my face with a handkerchief, I would be unaffected.

Wrong! Minutes later I awakened in the Magen Dovid Adom (Israeli Red Cross) annex near the Kotel.

As I understood it, the police had dragged me out after I had been overcome by the effects of the gas.

Within a half hour I was back at my Kotel Korner ready to officiate at the service.

The guests arrived, as did many other families for their respective Smachot. It was impossible to realize that minutes before, an unfortunate incident had transpired at this most holy site.

A Fast of Esther to remember!

Adult Bar Mitzvah

One would be amazed at how many adults, who never had a Bar/Bat Mitzvah as a teenager, opt to come to Israel for this ceremony. Better late than never!

Some are simple routine Bar Mitzvah services, where the pensioner--sometimes octogenarian--has his first Aliyah Torah honor and dons Tefilin for the first time.

He reaffirms his commitment to our religion and rededicates himself to our Torah.

A similar reaffirmation/reconsecration ceremony has been designed for grandmothers and often great-grandmothers.

But some ceremonies are especially memorable and unique:

(a) A 65 year old husband and wife, accompanied by his 91 year old mother, traveled to Jerusalem for the belated Bar Mitzvah. The elderly mother refused to die until she saw her son receive an Aliyah L'Torah (Torah honor) and an official Bar Mitzvah certificate.

(b) A 70+ year old celebrant was about to have his belated first aliyah. The wife, standing alongside the Mechitza separation fence, was sobbing hysterically. She explained to my wife, Ruby, that a half year ago he had had a massive heart attack and was clinically dead.

Through a medical miracle he was revived and now had regained his health.

During the recuperation period, he decided to have a long overdue Bar Mitzvah.

He wanted to express his thanksgiving, gratitude and appreciation to the Almighty for the gift of life that was restored to him. Jerusalem was the obvious choice as the most appropriate venue. Now witnessing this sentimental moment, the wife couldn't contain her emotions. Thus, the tears of joy!

(c) As a volunteer Rabbinical Council of America (RCA) Chaplain at the Hadassah Hospital Mount Scopus Cancer Hospice, I befriended one of the terminally ill patients. A bachelor, he confided in me that (1) he never had a Bar Mitzvah as a youngster and (2) he never had performed the Mitzvah of Tefilin.

When asked by me if he would like to have a belated Bar Mitzvah at the Kotel--if it could be arranged--he enthusiastically agreed. The dedicated Hospice staff of professionals and caring volunteers eagerly cooperated. Within a week we had made the necessary arrangements to transport this critically ill man from his hospital bed to the Wall.

It was a happening! He proudly wore his new Talit, a gift from friends. He placed Tefilin on his arm and head for the very first time. Tears of joy flowed from the guests' eyes as Reb Moshe recited the Torah blessings. We threw candy and danced with him in his wheelchair. I even had a Bar Mitzvah certificate prepared for the celebrant!

He asked to be taken near the Wall and to be left alone there for a few moments.

Everyone was overcome with deep emotion as they realized

the significance of this unique and powerful religious happening.

Unfortunately, one month later the same group gathered for his funeral!

During the Shiva, his sister told us how special the last weeks were for him. He retold each of his visitors every detail of his Kotel Bar Mitzvah and proudly showed off his certificate. That day at the Wall was his final and most wonderful life experience.

I have a picture of myself and Reb Moshe (as he was lovingly called) that sits on my desk.

I remember him daily. May his memory be for a blessing!

The Three Generational Bar Mitzvah

Over the years I have performed many father and son double Bar Mitzvah ceremonies.

I have performed mother and daughter Bat Mitzvah ceremonies. All are memorable.

But I will never forget my only three generational celebration that included also a grandfather!

A Russian family, now of Ohio, came to Israel for a Bar Mitzvah. The family had left the former Soviet Union and settled in America. God had been good to them and they prospered. They had become fully acculturated into American society.

It was time to celebrate a Bar Mitzvah in the family. They decided to have this milestone ceremony atop Masada.

Upon meeting the family at the hotel, the grandfather began to weep. He wanted me to be aware of how dangerous it was to have any religious rite in the Soviet Union. Consequently, he had no Bar Mitzvah nor did his son (the father of our Bar Mitzvah celebrant-to-be).

Now they are all free, living in freedom in the United States. They chose to come to the Holy Land for the first Bar Mitzvah in their family in many generations. I was deeply moved, listening to his tale of religious oppression, and now his excitement to have the privilege of seeing one of his descendants having a Bar Mitzvah.

I suggested that we should make this a three generational celebration. And so it was!

Grandfather (age 70), father (age 40), son (age 13).

Each donned a new matching Talit. Each celebrant wrapped Tefilin on his arm and placed Tefilin on his head. What an emotional moment to witness this awesome scene. We prayed and danced and cried together! Each got a certificate attesting to the fact that they had officially become a Bar Mitzvah.

Of all the thousands of ceremonies I have presided over, this is one service I will never forget. The impact of that religious experience was overwhelming. A powerful spiritual moment for Rituals Unlimited.

The Hawaiian Bar Mitzvah

New York grandparents called to arrange a Bar Mitzvah for their Jewish Hawaiian grandson. The grandfather was in Israel on business and asked to meet me to discuss the forthcoming family simcha.

He wanted me to know that the father of the celebrant--his son--was a non-believer and a non-practicing Jew. The family was reluctantly coming to Israel for this ceremony only to please the grandparents, who were also underwriting the entire trip.

"Ignore my son. He probably won't even shake your hand. He is hostile to Rabbis," the older gentleman embarrassingly confided. I was duly warned not to insist that the father wear Talit/Tefilin and not to give him any Torah honor.

The service was set for the Southern Wall Steps (of the Temple complex, around the corner from the Kotel.) It is an ideal venue, a perfect setting for a private serene service.

A few dozen guests joined the family for this celebration. The celebrant's father arrived and coldly walked past me without even making eye contact. He sat high up on the stairs and did not actively participate in any aspect of the service.

But I couldn't and wouldn't let this occasion pass without some aggressive gesture to reach out to this estranged, hostile Jew. I used all of my "A" material (See the Karzenism section) with a light humorous touch, in the finest tradition of Joyous Jewishness. It was certainly an upbeat service.

Following the formal prayers and my brief sermonette, we danced with the celebrant and it was a truly joyous Simchat Torah style celebration. It was a genuine Simcha.

As the men began removing their Tefilin, the father suddenly rose and started walking down the steps towards me. Everyone froze, including me not knowing what to expect.

And then.. he embraced me! He hugged me and began sobbing. He asked for permission to say a few words. With deep emotion he began to relate why he had become an atheist.

It seems that a few weeks before his own Bar Mitzvah, one of his grandmothers passed away. The family canceled the Simcha. It was rescheduled and another Haftorah had to be learned. Six months later, as he was to celebrate his Bar Mitzvah another death occurred in the immediate family and once again a cancellation.

He interpreted this as a sign from the Almighty. It was God's way of telling him that there was no place for him in Judaism. Hashem (God) was refusing to allow him to enter the adult congregation of Israel. All these years he had boycotted Judaism and only by accident did he marry a Jewish woman.

And now, in Jerusalem, he was watching his only son become

a Bar Mitzvah. He was listening to me explain the beauty of Judaism and he realized what he had missed all these years. He was publicly asking forgiveness from God and his family. Everyone was weeping as they listened to his moving monologue. He spoke for almost ten minutes and all of his words were recorded by the videographer.

I was so moved by his eloquence that I offered to fly to Hawaii and spend several weeks reintroducing him and the family to the beauty of traditional Torah Judaism. Half jokingly, I suggested that he send me a ticket and I would be on the next plane. (I carefully check my mailbox daily. It is now over five years, but I am patiently waiting for the invitation to become their private teacher).

You can never predict when a religious service or a sermon idea or some profound remark will affect a person so deeply. One never knows what might ignite the "Pintele Yid" (a spark within each Jew) to reawaken him/her to begin the journey that leads to a rediscovery of their Jewishness.

Funny E-mail (&Faxes): No More Snail Mail

Electronic Mail has become a part of our lives and Rituals Unlimited approaches the 21st Century with it's own home page and website. We are getting inquiries from literally all over the world, from Hong Kong to Hawaii and from Venezuela to Australia.. even from the Mauritius Islands! Here is a sampling of some of the questions we have received via Fax and E-mail.

1) Since we aren't a very religious family, is it possible to have a "non-religious Bar Mitzvah?" (Editors Note: A real oxymoron!)

2) Can we rent Tefilin for the service? We really do not wish to

spend the money to purchase something that will be used only once! (Editors Note:. Someone looking for a creative business venture might wish to consider opening a Tefilin rental agency. Avis or Hertz Rent-A-Tefilin!)

3) All the Tefilin we see in our local religious supply store are black. Our son doesn't like that color. Do you know of a store in Israel where we might purchase blue or red Tefilin? (his favorite colors)

4) Our son does not go to Religious School and cannot read Hebrew. We also are not Hebrew readers. Do you perform all English Bar Mitzvah services?

5) My son will not be 13 until December. We can only come to Israel this summer. Is it permissible to advance the ceremony a few months so that our child will have the opportunity of having an Aliyah at the Western Wall? (We could have come and not told you his real age!) Can you be flexible and stretch the religious law a bit for us?

6) We are planning a trip to Israel this summer and expect a rather large attendance for our son's Bar Mitzvah. We have many relatives and friends in your country. We wish to reserve the ENTIRE Kotel area for our Simcha. Will this be a problem for you to arrange?

7) I will be bringing my son to Israel next month with an organized tour program. We do not wish to miss anything from this comprehensive itinerary. I would like my son to have a symbolic Bar Mitzvah. If we come very early to the Wall, can we be back at the hotel to meet our tour group by 8 AM? P.S. My son does not know very much and cannot read Hebrew, so the service will have to be very short and simple. What do you charge for this type of abbreviated service?

8) We have scheduled a Bar Mitzvah with you this Summer and are now working out the list of honors for the Torah Service. We know that some are speaking and some non-speaking honors. Can you E-mail us a list of the most important non-speak-

ing honors. Can a non-Jew receive an honor? Also we have a Jewish atheist/agnostic who will be joining us. What would be the least offensive honor we could give him? Could he at least open the Ark doors? As you can see we will be a unique group!

9) In our Synagogue the Bat Mitzvah is encouraged to wear a Talit. At our Simcha next month, Amy intends to also wear a Talit. Should she purchase one here in our Sisterhood Gift Shoppe or do you recommend waiting and shopping for one in Meah Shearim? We were told that this colorful neighborhood has the largest selection in Jerusalem. Would you happen to know if they carry the pink striped Talit (with Kippa to match) in Jerusalem?

10) We were just told by a religious friend that our Bar Mitzvah service, you will be handling for us, is on what he called "Rosh Chodesh"—a special holiday—and the service is significantly longer. We are not particularly religious people and quite frankly have never before heard of this holiday. (Is it some sort of newly established Israeli observance?) We certainly don't want a long service! Can we abbreviate whatever is unnecessary and even skip those parts that allude to this unfamiliar holiday? We never observed it here at home and see no reason to start that day. Hope this won't be a major problem for you. We certainly hope that video and photography are allowed on the holiday of Rosh Chodesh!

11) My son knows that at the Bar Mitzvah they are going to throw candy at him. He is afraid of being hurt by hard candy. Some of his friends have been! I know that you supply the candy as part of your full service package. Could you kindly supply us with Marshmallows for Seth's Bar Mitzvah. We all would feel more relaxed knowing that he would be pelted with something soft.

12) Our tutor noticed that Brian's Bar Mitzvah, on the last day of Chanukah, requires an unusually long Torah Reading. Could you shorten it for him? We are Reform and all of our Torah readings are abbreviated! Thank you for your understanding and flex-

ibility. None of our guests will know the difference! They are all from a non-religious Kibbutz and know less than we do about the ritual procedures.

13) I know that skullcaps come in many varied colors. We are curious. Are there any specific colors expected at the Kotel at a Bar Mitzvah and is there any significance to the material from which the Kippot are made? We heard that many at Kotel only wear black velvet head coverings. We would really like a more festive bright color like blue. and made from satin. Will this be a problem?

14) Our travel agent told us that a Masada Bar Mitzvah does not require Tefilin.

We would really like our son to put on Tefilin at his Bar Mitzvah, which will be on that historic mountain. Please assure us that he will be able to wear the Tefilin at the service. As a Rabbi you certainly understand how important this is for us to have our son wear the Tefilin at least once in his life!

15) We have many important participants coming to our son's Bar Mitzvah— among them both grandfathers, a great grandfather, 2 great uncles, etc. We need Aliyot for all of them. We know that traditionally only 3 are distributed on a weekday. We are requesting an exception to this rule just for Randy's Bar Mitzvah because of the large group of VIP family members who will be traveling so far to join us for the Simcha. We need at least 7 Aliyot, possibly more. If you can accommodate us without violating any major religious law we would be grateful. If you cannot do so, we are requesting that you call 3 men for each aliyah and they will jointly recite the blessings.

Because of the special type of family we are I am sure that God will overlook these minor variations and bless you for your understanding in accommodating us.

68 OFF THE WALL

16) We have seen videos of some Bar Mitzvahs at the Wall and note that at some they lift the youngster on a chair and dance with him. We would like that also at Marc's Simcha. We do not have enough men to lift him on the chair. I know that you arrange for the Minyan when the family is small. Can you also arrange for strong men to help lift and dance with our son? If there is an extra charge for that service we will gladly cover it.

17) We have been told that at a Sephardic Bar Mitzvah some of the women make loud noises with their mouths and this adds to the festivity of the occasion. My question is twofold: Can we, an Ashkenazic family, have that tradition at our service? And if so can you arrange for one or more such ladies to be present to perform this task. We will gladly pay whatever the cost. Kindly find the best ladies available for this ceremony!

18) We have been warned that beggars often interfere with the service at the Wall by disturbing the guests who have come for the Bar Mitzvah. How can we keep them away from our corner? Do you have any suggestions?

19) We would like you to order and have 25 chairs set up for our guests at the Bar Mitzvah. Kindly make sure that all the chairs are the same color (we know that there are many types and different colors scattered around the Wall area). We are very particular that since a videographer will be filming the service everything will look perfect and fully color coordinated.

20) Is it possible to have a large sign made up with the name of our family on it. We do not know many of our Israeli relatives who will be coming to our Simcha They will have difficulty finding us and a sign would be helpful. How big could you make the sign?

21) Because our Bar Mitzvah is in the middle of August it could be extremely hot. Please rent a huge tent to cover our prayer area. I'm not sure if others do this, but we wouldn't mind being the first family to consider the comfort of our guests and provide such a convenience. What would this cost?

22) Following service at Wall we would like to serve a small Kiddush. We heard that the authorities do not encourage food to be served at the Kotel, but could we do so anyway? It would be a "simple" repast with soft drinks, wine, liquor, cakes, cookies, kichel, assorted fruits, pretzels, other noshery, etc. Could you, yourself, cater these post service refreshments or find someone to handle it for us?

23) We know that there is a custom to write a short prayer and place it within the cracks of the Wall. We wish to do this. Do the prayers have to be written in Hebrew?

24) Our son is frightened at having to carry the Torah in procession from the Ark to the reading table. He fears that if the Torah is too heavy and he drops it he will have to fast. He hates fasting! Could you make sure that you take the lightest Torah possible for him? Thank you in advance.

25) At the party, following the service, we know it is customary for the Bar Mitzvah to publicly recite the prayer over bread. Jason gets mixed up between the bread and wine blessings. Can

you assure him with an E-mail message that you will be there to prompt him before he has to recite this prayer and he need not worry?

26) We were wondering if it were possible to decorate our corner of the Kotel area along the Mechitza fence with balloons to make it appear more festive? If this seems sacrilegious, what about flowers? We want our Bar Mitzvah to be extra special and wonder if you could arrange this amenity for us?

27) We recently were told that a new custom has started at the Wall. Instead of putting small prayers inside the cracks, people are now placing money between the stones. Is this true? And if so, what is the suggested amount that is given?

28) We know that Tefilin are required at the Kotel. My son would like to only wear the hand Tefilin but omit the head piece since it will mess up his hair and he will look messy on the video and in the photographs. Will this be a problem?

29) Can two men share together the Hagbaah act of lifting the Torah? We have two cousins who we would like to honor with

this ceremony. Each would lift one of the wooden Torah rollers. Can you allow us to divide this honor?

30) Rabbi: We have a 3 part problem. You have been highly recommended to us as the #1 Rabbi in Israel to officiate at our son's Bar Mitzvah this July and we are extending an invitation to you to officiate. Here are the problems.

a) Our son will not be 13 until September
b) He refuses to wear Tefilin

We prefer him to read the same Torah portion as I did on my Bar Mitzvah rather than the weekly portion of this July. We feel it would be a wonderful bonding opportunity for father/son to read the identical verses from the Torah.

Hopefully none of the above problems are major ones that would prevent you from conducting our celebration.

31) Ashley's teacher is Reform. We are Conservative. Her teacher wants to know which prayers Ashley needs to know—the Reform or Conservative?

32) We just learned that it is proper to invite families with the name Cohen or Levy to the Bar Mitzvah. Is this true? We do not have anyone with these names among our close family or friends. If it is absolutely traditional to do this, could we ask you to locate people with these names who might be available to join us for the service?

Sam Orbaum's Masterpiece in The Jerusalem Post

I sent a sampling of some of the above E-mails to the popular Jerusalem Post columnist, Sam Orbaum. During the summer of 1997 he created the following humorous column in his "Off The Wall", which we have permission to repeat here for your enjoyment.

Nothing like a traditional Bar Mitzvah, marshmallows and all.

When Rabbi Jay Karzen made aliyah from Chicago in 1985, he discovered that the last thing the Jewish State needs is rabbis. Fortunately, he is just the right kind of rabbi to make his mark here: unorthodox Orthodox. After a year here, he found his calling. He couldn't help but notice the baalagon at the Wall, which for locals might be way of life, but for visiting families conscripting their children into Jewish adulthood, well, something had to be done.

The Bar Mitzvah King was born.

He called his shtick Rituals Unlimited, never realizing that hundreds of rituals later, he'd be writing a book on the "unlimited" part of it.

He's been asked to fulfill some of the darndest requests you can imagine. Like the 75 year old man who wanted a Bar Mitzvah. to please his 95 year old mother.

Some of the letters he's received suggest that there are Jewish youngsters (he also does a nice Bat Mitzvah) who might just as well be summoned to the Torah in Disneyland. An Arab beigele vender at Dung Gate understands more about Judaism, and the Wall, and Bar mitzvahs, than a fair slice of Diaspora Jewry.

Rabbi Karzen assures us that all these letters are real (I assure you his responses were a lot more kindly than my suggestions here under).

"We would like to decorate our side of the mechitza fence with balloons and flowers, to make it look more festive. Is this a problem?"

A problem? Nah. Regulars at the Wall have long been saying the place needs a bit of oomph. Maybe you can bring some Christmas decorations?

"We hear that most of the men wear black velvet skullcaps at the Wall. We prefer blue and intend to bring satin kippot with our son's name and date on them. Is this acceptable and will the ultra-Orthodox make fun of us if we wear yarmulkas of a different color and fabric?"

I assure you the ultra-Orthodox, who are avowedly not clothes-conscious, will be deeply moved by it all. In fact, I suggest you bring an extra supply of blue satin kipot for them to wear too. And I'll tell them to wear their blue suits.

"We expect a very large crowd at the Western Wall for our simcha. Can you please arrange to book the entire Kotel for this event? We are prepared. to pay what ever it costs".

Consider it done. I know of an abandoned disco downtown. We can redirect the other worshippers there for the day. Nobody will mind. PS: There is an automatic teller embedded in the Wall for your convenience.

"For our invitations we need to know the exact address of the Kotel."

The Wall, 3842-A The Holy One Blessed Be He Boulevard West, Suite 2428, al Quds.

"We are not a particularly religious family. Is it possible to have a non-religious BM ceremony at the Wall?"

Why, sure! A religious ceremony is not the only way to induct a blushing boy into manhood.

"Here in the USA all sets of Tefilin we see at the local Sisterhood Gift Shoppes are all BLACK. Can tefilin be blue or some other bright color? We would prefer something more festive than black! After all this is a Simcha!"

When you get to Israel, I'll take you to a Black Sisterhood Gift Shoppe where all the tefilin are white.

"Can you rent Tefilin in Israel? We do not wish to purchase this expensive item for one time usage."

Rent a car instead. A pair of tefilin is standard equipment with the rent-a-cars in Israel.

"Our son does not attend religious school and cannot read any Hebrew. Can you conduct an all-English Bar Mitzvah service for us?"

A cinch. We'll just use the original English version of the Torah and not the Hebrew translation.

"Jason's birthday is in November, but we can only come to Israel during the summer vacation. Is it permissible to advance the ceremony a few months? Can you be flexible and stretch the law a bit? After all, isn't it more important for a Jewish youngster to have his first aliyah in Jerusalem a few months early than not at all? (We could have lied and told you he was already 13.)

I could go to Rabbinical Prison for that. Tell you what we'll do. You say he'll be 12 years old? We'll give him a Bat Mitzvah instead.

"We will be part of an organized tour group and want to have a simple early morning Bar Mitzvah service in order to be back at the hotel for breakfast and not miss the day's tour. Can we have a 6:30 AM service (abbreviated?) Do we get a discount for a shorter service?"

Or you could skip the hotel breakfast, ask them for a discount, and I'll arrange for rabbis at the Kotel to serve coffee and danish.

"We plan to write prayers to place inside the Kotel, as is the tradition. Can these prayers be written in English or must they be only in Hebrew?"

I'm afraid the English translator is on vacation at present. Can you write them in Aramaic?

"Please order a large sign with our family name for the Kotel so that when the guests arrive they will be able to locate us easily."

Are you in luck. They've just installed a great new electronic cartoony kind of stadium scoreboard on the Kotel. We can program it to flash messages like "Yo! Gerald's Bar Mitzvah guest! Over here by the hotdog stand!"

"We are preparing the Torah honors list to bring with us. Can a non-Jew have a non-speaking honor during the Torah service? (i.e. open Ark curtain or doors) Will it be offensive to you if we give such an honor to a Jew who is an agnostic?"

I'm afraid this would not be allowed. They will have to convert. Fortunately, your Bar Mitzvah package includes five free circumcisions.

"Our travel agent has booked you to officiate at our daughter's Bat Mitzvah. She wishes to wear a talit for the service and we wish to purchase this item in Israel.

We understand that in an area called Meah Shearim they have the largest selection of Talitot. Do they also carry a variety of female talitot in feminine colors?"

You're more likely to find this item in Gaza City.

"I know that you supply the candy that is thrown at the Bar Mitzvah. Our son is afraid of being hurt by aggressive candy-throwers. Can we bring marshmallows from the States?"

May I suggest falafel balls?

Yasher Koach to Rabbi Karzen for sharing this stuff with us. Watch for his book, Off The Wall, coming to a Jewish bookstore or Sisterhood Gift Shoppe near you. Movie rights available on request.

Taxi to Kotel

I often take a taxi to the Kotel at the ungodly hour of 6 AM to prepare for my big Bar Mitzvah mornings. During one Chol Hamoed (intermediate day) Sukkot, on the day of the mass Birkat Kohanim, (Descendants of Aaron bless the throngs of assembled worshippers with the traditional priestly blessing) my cabdriver was not happy about driving into the Old City on such a busy traffic day.

I assured the cabby that it being so early, the traffic would be very minimal. He continued to complain and became abusive. As his first customer, I was ruining his day. He was non-stop in his criticism of religious Jews in general and me in specific, because I was demanding that he drive to the Kotel.

"I know you. You drive a red Mazda automobile. Why don't you drive yourself to the Kotel? All week long you don't call me to drive you around. Only today, when you don't want to get into traffic jams, you call me!"

He admonished me to recite an extra Al Chet (confessional) next Yom Kippur for the aggravation I was causing him. He wanted to take me only as far as the Jaffa Gate, but I refused to walk with all of the paraphernalia (Lulav and Etrog-Sukkot ritual equipment and Hebrew/English Siddurim, candy, extra Talitot, etc.) that I was carrying.

He had no choice but to continue on to the Kotel. There was absolutely no traffic at all at that early hour. When I exited the taxi he refused to take the 20 shekel bill that was due him. I insisted and left the money beside him on the seat.

He threw my money out of the cab onto the pavement and sped away! I gave the money to Tzadaka (charity) and tried hard to forget this most unpleasant incident—my only real negative Israeli taxi story. I have only the highest praise for our cabbies and have had some very special experiences riding in taxicabs in our country.

A few months later, I again had to call a taxi for an early morning Kotel service.

This time I had to also bring my own personal Sefer Torah scroll to the Wall because I had another service later on that morning at the Southern Wall Steps. At that venue one must bring ones own Torah and other equipment.

As you can already guess, who happened to answer my call?

The very same cabdriver who had given me so much of a hassle during Sukkot was once again destined to be my driver.

When he saw me now with a Sefer Torah, it blew his mind!

He had never before had a Torah scroll in his vehicle. This secular Jew was not only being asked to drive to his least favorite location, but also with a Torah!

There was very minimal conversation enroute. When we arrived at our destination, I was again prepared to pay the 20 shekel fee. Again he refused to accept my money.

"How can I take a fee from a man carrying a Sefer Torah?" he muttered.

I placed the 20 shekel bill alongside him and thanked him for the lovely, pleasant ride.

I often see him driving around town. I am anxiously awaiting my next encounter with him.

The Kotel Policeman and the Cellphone

Occasionally, when there is room, I get to park in the outside parking circle at the Kotel entrance. I had just completed three Bar Mitzvah services and was sitting in my car about to leave for home, when the cellphone rang—just as I had started to move the car away from the parking spot.

It is forbidden by law to drive while speaking into a portable phone (unless it is hooked into a speaker, which was not the case here). I was certainly not intending to break the law. I answered and told my wife that I'd be home in a few minutes. The conversation lasted only seconds.

But a policeman witnessed this violation of Israeli law. He demanded that I pull over (I was hardly moving—just backing my car slowly out of the parking circle) and show him my drivers license, automobile registration, insurance papers, etc. He was set to issue me a 750 shekel fine.

I pleaded with the policeman. I assured him that I never speak on my portable phone unless its connected to my speaker system. Invoking Jewish tradition, I reminded the officer that even the Almighty forgives. I apologized and admitted my transgression but begged him not to write this expensive ticket. Truthfully, I was more concerned about the four points on my record towards license revocation and possibly having to go to driver education school again.

As he proceeded to take out his ticket book, two of my friends, prominent tour guides, approached and joined a large crowd that had gathered to witness and enjoy this scene.

The guides, too, suggested to the policeman to forgive and forget. Even some of the onlookers implored the law enforcement officer to overlook my minor offense.

Suddenly, the policeman closed his ticket book and asked me to follow him. He pointed to a half dozen beggars standing nearby. "Go and give each of them Tzadakah," (charity) he insisted. I ran and generously gave to each of them.

"Okay, I will overlook what you did this time. But never again even answer the cellphone unless its connected to your car speaker," he warned.

I blessed him and almost kissed him. What a wonderful gentleman he was. I now see him often. I never fail to remind him of his kindness and how I never speak on the cellphone while driving. He smiles. We are now buddies. We warmly greet each other whenever we meet. Truly one of Jerusalem's finest!

The UJA Group and Netilat Yadayim

Several times a year, Ruby and I are invited to join one of the visiting United Jewish Appeal (UJA) Missions for a Shabbat Eve dinner at a local hotel. We provide the Ruach (spiritual joy) for the tourists and conduct a Sabbath experience for them.

We sing with them the traditional prayers at the Shabbat table, recite the Kiddush (sanctification over a goblet of wine) and recite the blessing over the Challah bread.

During dinner we sing Zmirot (hymns) and finally the Birkat Hamazon. (Grace after meal)

In addition, we have an opportunity to socialize with the guests and give them a taste of Shabbat in Jerusalem.

One Shabbat, at dinner in the King David Hotel, I was doing my usual thing with a small California UJA delegation. We were ready to recite the Hamotzie blessing over the challah. I announced that before cutting and breaking bread, I was going to perform the ritual act of Netilat Yadayim (washing of the hands) and invited everyone, who wished, to join me.

For this ceremony, the hotel had placed a large silver bowl in our private dining room.

With cup in hand, I proceeded to wash each hand as is the tradition. It was evident that none of these people had ever seen this ritual performed. I asked if I might assist each of them to also wash their hands. They all nodded and I helped them pour water over each of their hands. We then recited the appropriate blessing together.

As we were walking back to the table, I overheard one lady remark to her husband:

"It would be nice for us to introduce this ceremony back home, but where would we find a Rabbi to come and wash our hands"?

This is similar to the apocryphal story of the young eager-to-be-religious girls witnessing the same ceremony. There is a rule that when washing the hands before a meal no ring be worn. Many remove their wedding band and place it between their teeth for a few seconds of the Netilat Yadayim. The young girl lamentably says to her friend: "We will not be able to do this ceremony yet because we don't have a ring to place between our teeth."

The Lady and the Mechitza

Travel agents often invite me to deliver talks before organized tour groups.

I was once discussing the Orthodox views of "Conversion to Judaism" with senior citizens from abroad, here on a study/tour program. They asked me all sorts of questions on various miscellaneous topics related to the general issue of religious pluralism in Israel.

One hostile lady challenged me as to why men and women were separated during prayer in the Orthodox Synagogues. "Why must women be second class citizens in Shul?" she defiantly asked.

I explained that the purpose of separate seating and the Mechitza (partition between the sexes) was for a different reason. Prayer requires devotion! (Kavana) When we pray we must feel as if we are standing in the very presence of the Almighty. We owe Him total concentration and devotion.

I continued. "Any normal male who sees a lovely lady next to him cannot help but be distracted. Our eyes will automatically shift from the prayerbook to the female near him. In this competition between God and the beautiful member of the opposite sex, the Almighty will be the loser. Our Rabbis recognized this fact of life, and to prevent it from occurring, separated the sexes during times of prayer".

The woman who asked the question was not particularly attractive. She insisted that my explanation was unacceptable and nonsense.

In response, I stared at her and said: "Madam, if you were sitting next to me, I would have a hard time concentrating on my prayers"... She blushed, smiled and wasn't heard from again that night. I think I made her day!

"Korim" in the Great Synagogue

The Jerusalem Great Synagogue is one of the most beautiful Houses of Worship in the Jewish world. The Shabbat and Holiday services attract worshippers from every continent. I am proud to be one of the regulars, who enjoys their great world class Cantor and the equally outstanding male choir.

Though a strictly Orthodox Synagogue, many Conservative, Reform, Reconstructionist and secular Jews come to participate in the glorious musical service, especially on the major holidays.

One Yom Kippur, a non-religious secular Jewish Texan came to worship in the Great Synagogue. He sat next to me and asked a number of questions throughout the service.

It was obviously his first experience in an Orthodox congregation. He seemed to enjoy the dovening and the "magnificent heavenly melodies" (as he referred to it) of the Chazzan and choir.

It was now time for the "Korim"—that special part of the Musaf (additional prayer) liturgy where the congregants all kneel and prostrate before the Almighty. This was something that he had certainly never seen before. He had assumed that Jews were forbidden to get down on their knees and bow to God.

"I thought that only Catholics do that!"

I was his Rebbe for the day and gave him a running commentary of what we were doing and why we were doing it. He asked me if he could also join in the Korim ceremony. He joined me in the aisle as we began the Avodah (Temple Sacrifice) segment of the Musaf with its numerous kneeling requirements. He was now really into this Yom Kippur happening!

"Are we looking for anything while we are down here?" he asked.

He stayed through Neilah (final Yom Kippur service) until the Shofar (Ram's Horn) was sounded. I am not sure if he fasted, but this was his most intense High Holiday. He thanked me for having taken the time and patience to explain so much throughout the day. "I learned more about Judaism in these few hours than at any other period of my life."

Wherever this man is now, I hope he never forgets his day with me in the Jerusalem Great Synagogue. I will never forget him!

Children's Creative Biblical Insights

The following adorable piece came over the internet and are said to have been written by actual students and are genuine, authentic and are not retouched or corrected. Enjoy and smile!

In the first book of the Bible, Guinness's, God got tired of creating the world, so he took the Sabbath off.

Noah built an ark, which the animals came into by pears.

Noah's wife was called Joan of Ark.

(Author's note: The Midrash relates that her name was actually Naamah.)

Lot's wife was a pillar of salt by day but a ball of fire by night.

Moses led the Hebrews to the Red Sea where they made unleavened bread—which is bread without any ingredients.

The Egyptians were all drowned in the dessert.

Moses went up on Mount Cyanide to get The Ten Ammendments.

The first commandment was when Eve told Adam to eat the apple.

The fifth commandment is to humor thy father and mother.

The seventh commandment is thou shalt not admit adultery.

Moses died before he reached Canada.

Joshua led the battle of Geritol.

The greatest miracle in the Bible is when Joshua told his son to stand still and he obeyed him.

David was a Hebrew king, skilled at playing the liar. He fought the Finkelsteins, a race of people who lived in Biblical times.

King Solomon had 300 wives and 700 porcupines.

The Jews are a proud people and throughout history had trouble with the Genitals.

Karzen Vs. Richard Tucker

Let me backtrack several decades. I always wanted to be a Rabbi! Some youngsters aspire to become policemen or fireman. Jewish youngsters fantasize about a career as a surgeon or corporate attorney. My family insists that as a youngster I played "rabbi-cantor." A towel was draped over my shoulder, as if wearing a Talit, (prayer shawl) and I walked around the house chanting and praying. By age 8, I was the child soloist in the local synagogue choir and also accompanied the Cantor to hundreds of weddings that he solemnized with his colorful and melodious choir-boy ensemble.

My first High Holiday cantorial post was at a small Chicago Orthodox Synagogue. Billed as the 18 year old "Wonder" Cantor, some of my comedian friends used to say, when they saw the newspaper and billboard advertisements, that what these ads really meant —come and hear Karzen and you will then wonder if he is a real Chazzan. (Cantor)

That year the world famous operatic superstar, Richard Tucker, was serving as the Cantor at a nearby prestigious Synagogue. He was my competition! "Wonder" Cantor Jay Karzen vs. the world renowned Metropolitan opera star-cantor. Need I say who had the larger attendance?

It was SRO in his Congregation, but a significant number of their worshippers came to listen to my chanting and make the inevitable comparison. One visitor even made a point of approaching the Amud (Cantorial pulpit) and offered me a ticket suggesting that I go and listen to a "real" Chazzan!

He was right. This gentleman indirectly convinced me to be a Rabbi and leave the chanting to professional artists. To this day I enjoy "dovening" (praying) for the Congregation, and often do so — but only as a non-professional Baal Tefilah. (layman cantor)

Chief Rabbi at Age 25

Ottumwa, Iowa? Where is it? Are there Jews in Ottumwa?
Seventy five families became my first Congregation and at age twenty three, had the honor of being proclaimed "Chief Rabbi" (and only Rabbi!) of Southeastern Iowa.

My Rebettzin (title for Rabbi's wife), Ruby, and I have nostalgic memories of 1959-62 as our growth years They were the learning years to prepare us for other challenges that were to follow. We have never forgotten the kindness shown to us by so many of the warm and beautiful families that comprised our very first Congregation. The special friendships that were forged and the unique people that touched our lives stay with us until this day.

Our two children, now of Efrat and Hebron, were born in Ottumwa. What a Zchut (merit) for this obscure community!

What? Me Make a Mistake in the Torah Reading?

An incident occurred on our very first official Shabbat (Sabbath) in Ottumwa that remains indelibly etched in my memory.

By necessity, the Rabbi was required to serve also as the Baal Koray. (Torah Reader) The President suggested that the Torah Service be performed as quickly as possible.

In my haste to read swiftly, my eyes leaped ahead of my lips and I erred in reading an important word from the Scroll. As in any typical Congregation, there is always one or more persons anxious to correct the Baal Koray by yelling out the proper word.

(I have never been sure if this was to guarantee that the Torah reading would be flawless and perfect and thus the congregants would fulfill their obligation of hearing a Kosher Kriat HaTorah (proper Torah Reading) or if this was a type of sadism to embarrass the reader.)

An elderly gentleman—the only knowledgeable worshipper among those present-proceeded to call out the correct word. Immediately, the president, standing at my side, looked out in anger at this learned Jew sitting in the second row and rebuked him publicly. Pointing a finger at him, he yelled: "Now, you be quiet! If our Rabbi says that's the word, then that's the word!"

And amazingly, in the three years I served the Ottumwa community, I NEVER AGAIN MADE A MISTAKE IN THE TORAH READING!

Praying for Strawberries

A young Rabbi, fresh out of the Yeshiva (Rabbinical College), prays that no question will be asked of him that might embarrass, or worse, stump him. The first such inquiry was asked almost immediately after arriving in Ottumwa.

One of the matriarchs of the community inquired if we might reinstate that important special pre-High Holiday service that had not been recited for many years in Ottumwa. She remembered that her pious father would rise early in the morning before the Jewish New Year to pray for the Strawberries! She was wondering if that special ritual might also be on my agenda.

Pray for the strawberries? Not quite sure how to handle such a delicate, sensitive question, I told her that the Ritual Committee had not planned on conducting this specific service this season, but possibly next year it would be considered. I reasoned that we could have an entire year to research this strange request and discover what exactly is the "strawberry service."

I wrote to former classmates and other scholarly colleagues. Needless to say, none had heard of such a strawberry ritual. No one could help. Obsessed, I would not rest until this perplexing puzzle was resolved. And then, as if a bolt of Talmudic lightening had suddenly hit me, it became so obvious...

This women's father had gone to the Synagogue early on the eve of Rosh Hashanah (The Jewish New Year) for Selichot. (The Penitential Service) One of the most prominent prayers of that lengthy service is called "Zchor Briss." (Literally: Remember The Covenant) If you say those two words, Zchor Briss, quickly, it sounds like strawberries (prerequisite... European Yiddish accent)" Zchor Briss! Zchor Briss!" (Try it! It certainly does sound like strawberries)... To her ears, as a young girl, it sounded as if her father was praying for the strawberries... Unfortunately, we never did have a Zchor Briss service!

It is now many decades later and to this day when we reach that beautiful section of the liturgy, erev (eve of) Rosh Hashanah, and I ask the Almighty to "remember the covenant" (Zchor Briss) I must confess a little secret—I also ask God to bless the world's strawberry crop! I think that my Ottumwa friend, who is now in Paradise, would be very pleased!

The Cinerama Prayerbook

A year later, having solved the Zchor Briss/Strawberry mystery, a woman called to inform me that her grandmother was visiting from New York and would be at Sabbath services. She wanted me to arrange for the special "Cinerama" prayerbook that her octogenarian Bubbe (grandmother) regularly used during her prayers.

Ready for any similar mis-pronunciation. I was determined that never again would I have to agonize over having to decipher corrupted and/or misunderstood Hebrew words.

The caller was referring to the once popular Yiddish translation of the traditional prayerbook called "Tzennu U'renna" (literally translated: Go Out and See) Again, if you say the words quickly it might sound like Cinerama. Older readers and theater-goers might remember the Cinerama craze of the sixties. How easy then for someone unfamiliar with this Hebrew/Yiddish Siddur (prayer book), to hear the words Tzenna U'renna and internalize it as Cinerama.

Unfortunately, I had no copy of this prayerbook in my study, nor did the Congregation have one in its modest library. Many decades have passed. The New Yorker has long gone to her eternal reward. I now have a copy of this wonderful Yiddish prayerbook to give this lady when we meet again after the Mashiach (Messiah) comes.

Questions Asked by Non-Jews

By necessity, I was very involved in interfaith activity. The Synagogue regularly hosted church groups who came to visit and listen to a talk on Judaism by the Rabbi. They were interested in what Jews believe; the similarities and differences between Judaism and Christianity; why we don't accept Jesus as the Messiah; why we don't celebrate Christmas and Easter, etc.

A Question and Answer period always followed the presentation. Here are some of the unbelievable questions that were asked:

1) Is it true that at a Jewish wedding all the men must remove their glasses and break them?

2) Do men wear skullcaps to hide the small horns growing on their heads?

3) Why do Jews celebrate a holiday about Russia? (They were referring to Rosh Hashanah which sounds like Russia Shana)

4) Can you explain why Jews are forbidden to eat Young Kip-

pers? (Alluding to the Fast of Yom Kippur, The Day of Atonement)

5) If "Be fruitful and multiply" is a commandment, why do Jews have to wear prophylactics each day? (The black leather ritual Tefillin worn on weekday mornings by observant Jewish men is often referred to as phylacteries.)

6) If Jews are forbidden to eat any pork product, why is there a ceremony called "Pig In A Pen?" (The reference was obviously to the redemption of the first born son, known as the Pidyon Haben).

7) Can a Jewish boy have a BAT Mitzvah and a girl, a BAR Mitzvah, if they so choose? (Bar Mitzvah is the ceremony celebrating a 13 year old BOY reaching religious maturity. Bat Mitzvah is the commemoration of a 12 year old GIRL reaching religious maturity.)

8) Is there any significance to the different colored skull caps?

9) If a Rabbi is like the Jewish priest, can he marry?

10) If Jesus was a Jew, did he have a Bar Mitzvah?

Merry Xmas Rabbi!

One early, wintry, snowy morning, I was stopped by a local policeman for a possible traffic violation. Upon scrutinizing my driver's license and realizing that I was Ottumwa's "Jewish" Rabbi, he apologetically returned my document and sincerely wished me: "Merry Christmas, Rabbi."

My First Funeral Blunder

An embarrassing mistake occurred while officiating at my first funeral in Ottumwa. A pillar of the Congregation had passed away. Nervously, I was delivering my first eulogy in the presence of the entire Jewish community and numerous non-Jews.

Suddenly, in the midst of the memorial service, I referred to the deceased by the wrong name! Instead of his first name, which was Louis, I called him Herbert — the name of his younger nephew, sitting in the first pew!

After the crowd's collective gasp, I immediately realized the error. From that moment on —for all of my rabbinical career —I always wrote the name of the deceased in large letters and placed it in front of me so that I would never ever repeat that embarrassing blunder.

P.S. A year later, Herbert suddenly died and I had my second funeral.

P.S.S. Under the Chuppah (marriage canopy) I also placed the names of the bride and groom in large letters in my rabbinic manual, to assure that I would not err in their names. During one of my first wedding ceremonies I proclamed the bride and her father, husband/wife. It never happened again.

The Electric Spinning Rooftop Draydel

The Ottumwa community consisted of 75 families—200 souls—among a population of 34,000. Christmas season was most difficult for our people. From a business perspective the season was a gift from God. Ottumwa was the county seat and the major shopping area for over 45,000, in southeastern Iowa. However, from the spiritual point of view, December made every Jew aware of his minority status.

One scene still haunts me: A most prestigious family in our community wanted to honor me with "throwing the switch" to light their Chanukah holiday display. The minor Jewish Holiday of Chanukah (celebrating the rededication of the ancient Temple in Jerusalem in 165 B.C.E.) occurs also in December. Just as the President of the United States lights the official Christmas tree in Washington, they had designed and erected a Chanukah scene on their rooftop-an elaborate spinning Sevivon/Draydel (a top with Hebrew lettering) all electrified and truly spectacular—unlike anything ever seen before.

Here was an obvious attempt to imitate the non-Jewish custom of decorating and illuminating their home for this holiday. The family felt the need to copy their non-Jewish neighbors, but with a Jewish theme. They wanted me to have the "kovod" (honor) of officially blessing their home erev Chanukah with the throwing of the switch!

It is now many decades later. I am embarrassed to admit that I was there to perform the ceremony of launching the only spinning rooftop draydel in the community and possibly the world. May the Almighty forgive me!

Tuesday Night at the Movies

In spite of our busy-ness— that now included two children who required full-time attention, my interfaith work, teaching, studying and sermon preparation, my wife, Ruby, and I cleared the calendar every Tuesday Evening for the MOVIES. The management of the theater chain that operated the two movie houses in the city gave all clergymen free passes to both theaters. We often attended both movies on our big weekly night out.

One wintry January, a massive snowstorm fell and blanketed the city. Because we lived on a high hill it was impossible to drive on our street. Most of the businesses closed early due to the weather conditions. But it was Tuesday and our night for the movies! We called to make sure that the theater remained open and then set out on foot so as not to miss our regular "date!"

In five foot snow drifts, we managed to arrive at the theater. We were the ONLY customers to venture out on such a miserable winter night. Like the old joke: (Q)" When does the movie start"? (A)"How fast can you get here?" The manager held the movie for us. They knew we were coming (it was Tuesday and the Rabbi and Rebettzin always attend on this night) and they did screen the film(s) for us—free pass and all! We bought lots of candy and cokes so as to at least allow them some "profit!"

The "Bluffer" Rebbe

From being Chief Rabbi of Ottumwa and environs, it was time to move to Council Bluffs, Iowa—at the other end of the State. If I was the Ottumwa Rebbe, would I now become the "Bluff"er Rebbe?

In 1962 we moved to Council Bluffs in Southwest Iowa, near Omaha, Nebraska, where we would serve for three additional years in the "boonies." The Jewish population of Council Bluffs was approximately the same size as Ottumwa and the Synagogue "parsonage", which we named the "Bet HaRav" (literally: the Rabbi's House), was truly majestic. Legend has it that it was constructed for the famous Civil War General Dodge . It was a Southern ante-bellum style, white mansion set upon a hill with a surrounding porch. Our home was situated on a half block of prime real estate property! We often had parties, gatherings and numerous meetings in this house. It became the show place for the Jewish community.

Ours was the only house on the block without a Christmas tree, but the only house with a Sukkah. (The outdoor hut used during the Festival of Sukkot/Tabernacles.)

Kelev, the Dog, is Dead!

My first major mini-crisis occurred within weeks of our arrival. One of the most influential citizens, a prominent political figure and pillar of the Jewish community, called to inform me that his DOG had just died. He had no children and this dog was his "baby." He was very emotionally involved with this animal. and the death was a traumatic experience for him and his wife. He was not calling to invite me to officiate at the funeral but to inform me that he was intending to say Kaddish (prayer for the dead) for his departed pet. He was requesting that at Shabbat morning service I chant the "El Maley Rachamim" (literally: The Lord Who Is Full of Compassion... the special memorial prayer) for his beloved departed "Kelev."

I am sure that I was absent from the Yeshiva when we learned how to handle such situations. I do not recall any responsa literature regarding this type of case nor do I recollect my Rosh Yeshiva (Chief Rabbi of the Rabbinical Seminary) ever discussing such a possibility. What does one do? What would you do?

I told him that I have a substitute prayer for animals because it would not be proper to recite the very same prayer in memory of Kelev as for one's parents. He was very receptive to my words of consolation. I demonstrated compassion and understanding for his grief and did not ridicule his request. Because I offered to recite an alternate prayer, (which I had to compose) he became my close friend and supporter.

P. S. Rabbis are often asked to officiate at "funerals" for a variety of animals, i.e. turtles, hamsters, birds, etc. They are private, brief memorial services when parents wish to comfort their children on the death of a pet. The above Kelev incident was the first of many that followed through the years.

Tying the Knot or Going to the Dogs

On one specific occasion I recall being asked to officiate at a "wedding" for two dogs, one female/one male, who were purchased as pets. The children refused to have them live together without a marriage ceremony. With ingenuity and creativity, a simple original ceremony was performed... No Halacha (Jewish law) violated! So help me, its true!

Over the years I officiated at many "funerals" for pets. I blessed new autombiles, bicycles and snowmobiles. I conducted Chanukat Habayit (dedication of new home) ceremonies for homes and businesses. The scope of the variety of ceremonies Rabbis are asked to perform is unlimited. You may have already guessed that the concept of "Rituals Unlimited" was being conceived.

The Oneg Tuesday Prison Caper

Unexpectedly, I received a call from one of the Iowa prisons. A Jewish inmate was seriously ill and requested to see a Chaplain of his own faith. I drove the several hundred miles to pay a pastoral call on a fellow Jew who was in need. As long as a Rabbi was to visit, it was decided to also include a brief prayer service in the chapel for the other Jewish inmates. The Sisterhood sent me off with care packages of mandel bread, kichel, sponge cake and other Jewish delicacies for our "Oneg Tuesday" (The term "Oneg Shabbat" refers to the repast often served in Synagogues after the conclusion of Sabbath services).

While the official prison census listed only a half dozen members of our faith, several dozen attended the afternoon service. It is amazing how a religious reawakening can occur when free refreshments are advertised. Each attendee claimed to have a Jewish relative. We didn't have a kosher minyan but we did doven! Adding a number of popular prayer songs to our service, like "Adon Olom" and "Ayn Kaylohaynu", it evoked a positive response by the authentic Jewish inmates and it was heartwarming that they remembered the traditional melodies.

Now comes the incredible part of the story. We concluded our service/social hour and it was time to visit the inmate-patient. Luckily, one of the participants at my service, dressed in a white medical jacket, volunteered to escort me to the patient. This kind and seemingly very concerned "doctor" gave me the full medical background and related the detailed life history of the man.

I spent a half hour with the gravely ill patient. He wanted to make peace with God before he passed away. He felt the need to confess the sins of his not so ideal lifestyle and be assured that the Almighty would indeed forgive him if he repented and did Teshuva. (term denoting sincere repentance) We prayed together and it felt good knowing that a fellow Jew could die with peace of mind.

The "doctor" waited patiently outside the room during the private session with the dying prisoner. How impressed I was that this institution had in its employ such a caring staff . The State of Iowa was to be commended on its dedicated personnel.

My white-jacketed friend then offered to escort me to the parking lot. I assured him that there was no need for this. Thanking him for the time he spent with me, I told him that I would write a letter of commendation to the Warden praising this most dedicated member of the staff. He insisted on walking me to my automobile and nothing that I said would change his mind.

As soon as we reached the exit to the parking area, two hefty security guards immediately appeared to prevent my escort from leaving the building. It seems that my companion friend was not a doctor.. and was not even on the staff at all. He was one of the prisoners, knowledgeable of the medical vernacular, who enjoyed "playing doctor." The guards apologized to me and hoped that he hadn't been too much of a "nudnik" (pest) .They didn't use that precise word but that was the gist of it. This was a Jimmy Cagney movie come true and I was the foil for a possible attempted prison breakout!

That night, after safely arriving home, there was a movie on TV—most coincidental— of a chaplain being taken hostage at the local state penitentiary.

Having a Ball in Beersheba

It was during my tenure in this community in the Summer of 1964 that we made our first of twenty five pilgrimages to Israel. Two memorable episodes make us chuckle to this day.

While traveling with a group of American tourists, our itinerary required a two night stay in Beersheba, the capitol of the Desert, the Negev. We arrived at a newly-built hotel and we were among their first guests.

We were warmly welcomed by the hotel manager himself. He apologized for the fact that the newly installed elevator was not yet in operation. Since Ruby and I were the youngest couple, he assigned us the room on the top floor as it would easier for us to carry the luggage up the six flights. No bellhops were in sight!

The manager also informed us that not every room had a bathtub or shower, Some did not have the closets completed. But he did boast of this rapidly developing southern city. He detailed how the new hotel would increase tourism. Just months before only sand could be seen in every direction and suddenly this new building boon. His enthusiasm and excitement was infectious. We were made to feel a part of the modern history of Beersheba. Who cared if there were proper bathtubs, showers or closets?

We shlepped (dragged) our heavy luggage up to the sixth floor and entered the room—the first occupants. The manager forget to mention that the air conditioning was not operative nor were the telephones connected. The room was "closetless", but there was a bathtub and shower stall!

I hurriedly rushed down the steps to inquire if there was a room with air-conditioning. It was to be connected in a week, the apologetic manager explained. But he assured me that as long as the room had a shower, we should be satisfied because some of the rooms didn't even have that.

Up the six flights I ran. We were the lucky ones, I reasoned. We have both a shower and bathtub! However, there was no place to hang the wrinkled clothes.

Down again I ran to ask if perchance there were hangers available. The manager took a liking to me. I wasn't complaining— merely requesting— and he felt sorry that I was running up and down the six floors so frequently. He told me that he would personally bring up a small closet with hangers on condition that I wouldn't tell the other guests in our group.

Within the hour we had our "closet". More correctly, it was two chairs and four hangers! How can a Zionist compare the lack of such unimportant conveniences when we had a spectacular view of the newly developing city of Beersheba?

Netanya's Chassidic Paradise

On that same trip we had the privilege of being among the first guests at a Chassidic resort hotel in Netanya. We checked into our modest room and soon noticed that the shower stall did not have a proper curtain. I called the front desk and inquired as to whether we might have a shower curtain brought to our room. The polite clerk informed us that they did not have such luxuries, but added that the hotel did not expect the guests to clean the floor following a shower! How can one respond to such a statement?

It was shower time! The floor in the bathroom was not level. As I began to shower, the water was flooding not only the bathroom floor, but also into the bedroom under the closed door, due to the uneven surface. The rug was already floating, as were our shoes!

Again calling the on-duty clerk about our predicament, we were told not to be concerned, the maid would come immediately to tidy up the room. And, indeed, she did arrive promptly. She offered to wait until both our showers were completed, since we would obviously require her services again.

If one can muster a sense of humor about these absurdities..... the hotel itself, the food, the religious character, the view of the Sea, etc. were very special. Our two days there were memorable! We have since traveled extensively and stayed in many beautiful deluxe hotels around the world. Yet none of these 5 star hotels are etched in our memory. But the Chassidic hotel in Netanya will always remain a nostalgic highlight of our first pilgrimage to the country that would eventually be our permanent home.

Hava Nagila at Yad Vashem

We had just concluded an emotional visit to Israel's powerful Holocaust Museum, the Yad Vashem. Upon leaving the Hall of Remembrance, everyone in the group was wiping away tears.

A lovely, elderly woman was emotionally moved and wanted to do something "Jewish." She suggested that we all clasp hands and sing Hava Nagila (Literal meaning: Come Let Us Rejoice). She began to sing, and others, assuming it was the correct and proper thing to do, joined her. Suddenly, everyone was singing this joyous Hebrew song on the memorial grounds of Yad Vashem. Within seconds everyone was also dancing. How strange it must have appeared.

In retrospect, maybe the answer to all of our enemies, is to dance and sing such songs as Hava Nagila. For in truth, long after all of our enemies have disappeared off the face of the earth, the Jewish people will still be singing the joyous Hava Nagila and Am Yisrael Chai. (The People of Israel Lives!)

De "Plainer" Rebbe

In 1965, after six years in Iowa, we moved back to the Chicagoland area for what was to become my major rabbinic pulpit. For 22 years we served the Des Plaines, Illinois Jewish community and created a flourishing community that, at its peak, numbered over 500 affiliated families.

We had come back to the Chicago area so that our two school age children could attend Day School. A new community was developing in the Des Plaines area, a Synagogue was being formed and I was chosen to be the first spiritual leader of the Maine Township Jewish Congregation.

After we arrived, I looked over the corn fields and envisioned a thriving Jewish Kehillah (community) which would some day be a role model of an ideal, dynamic Torah community.

I Am Triplets

When prospective members would ask "What denominational Rabbi are you? Orthodox, Conservative of Reform?" I would respond: "I'm triplets! I'm all three!" And then I'd explain...

"I am Orthodox (which comes from the Greek meaning "right path" -orthos doxo) because I, indeed, try to walk in the right path; Conservative, because I believe in conserving our beautiful religion; Reform because I want to reform those Jews who have lost the way"

Patiently, I explained to each new family that my aim is to re-introduce the community to the splendor of Judaism! Many were duly impressed with our enthusiasm and gave the new emerging Synagogue a chance!

During discussions regarding religious beliefs, invariably the statement would be made: "Rabbi, I am not a religious Jew!" I would respectfully respond by asking them to kindly add the one word -YET - and would insist that they say: "I am not a religious Jew YET! One never knows today what might transpire tomorrow. Today you aren't (yet) religious, but who knows what tomorrow will bring."

It is difficult to argue that point!

Home of Joyous Jewishness

An approach to Judaism known as Joyous Jewishness was created!

Ruby and I developed this creative philosophy because we found the adjectives used before the word Jew (Orthodox, Conservative, Reform) to be deceptive. We all recognize so-called Orthodox Jews (with the big O) who, while they may observe ritual commandments meticulously, are inconsistent in their personal ethical and moral practices and cause Chillul Hashem. (Desecration of God's Name) There are Jews who prefer the big "C" or "R" (Conservative/Reform) and faithfully observe Kashrut (Dietary Laws) and other Mitzvot (Commandments)

If one HAS to use an adjective, choose "Joyous" because one should enjoy being a Jew and take pleasure in the performance of Mitzvot, customs and traditions of Yiddishkeit (Judaism). We sought to impart an infectious excitement revolving around the Sabbath and holidays, the Synagogue and everything that is part and parcel of our religion. This is the brand of Judaism we packaged for the new Congregation.

A "Nooj"

During one of the adult education lectures describing the major denominations of Judaism, a question was raised: Could one could legitimately be called an Orthodox Jew if he were not fully observant and unable, as an example, to properly observe the Sabbath and Dietary Laws, etc.

I maintained that if one accepted the basic fundamental belief of Orthodoxy—namely, Divine Revelation— that the Torah was given by the Almighty, —then even if he was not (yet) religiously observant, he is entitled to be called Orthodox. But I suggested that such a Jew be called a "NOOJ." (Non Observant Orthodox Jew)

Most Jews rightly assume that being Orthodox implies a commitment to maximum observance of all the 613 Commandments of our Torah. Since many Jews have altered and discarded many ritual Mitzvot and do not always achieve their "Jewish Best" my Joyous Jewishness became, and still is, very appealing. It is an ideal solution for those who feel the unnecessary need to describe themselves with an adjective.

Joyous Jewishness attracted followers because it made Judaism enjoyable. As the psalmist said: SERVE THE LORD WITH JOY! COME BEFORE HIM WITH SINGING (Psalm 100) People were attracted to this simple, non-complicated philosophy that we were popularizing.

We sang many Chassidic niggunim (melodies) at our services and from all over Chicgaoland people flocked to us to celebrate holidays like Simchat Torah (joyous holiday at the conclusion of the Sukkot Festival on which the annual Torah Reading cycle is completed). There was no more joyous place to be in the entire area than in Maine Township Jewish Congregation for this yomtov. (holiday) The specialness of this holiday and ecstasy that was generated lingered long after the holiday had past. Our talented Religious School music teacher even composed our holiday theme song: "Chag Somayach means Happy Holiday!" which is sung around the world to this day. It was the unofficial anthem of our Shul (Synagogue) and to this day when reminiscing, the song invariably finds its way into the conversation..

House Calls Can be Dangerous!

A meeting was arranged with a young woman in the privacy of her home, regarding her impending divorce. Upon arrival, I was non-plussed to note that she was dressed quite immodestly. She insisted that we be seated together in front of the picture window, where from the street one could see clearly into the room.

I was anxious to leave there as quickly as possible, feeling uneasy. She seemed to be prepared for a lengthy visit, insisting on serving an alcoholic beverage, which I politely refused. During the course of my explanation regarding the importance of a religious divorce—the "Gett"— she happened to mention that her "ex" threatened to kill her should she be found with another man.

Here I was sitting in front of a large window, visible from the street! I envisioned the husband driving past the house, observing us and assuming that I was her lover/ boyfriend and shooting us both in a fit of rage.

Looking at my watch I informed my hostess of a pressing engagement and was out the door in record time. I vowed never again to make an unaccompanied house call to a female member!

Beware of 23rd Psalm in Winter

Even in death, there is often a light side and unpredictable funny situations occur. Isn't it a bit strange that the first three letters of funeral are FUN?

On one occasion while conducting a graveside service in sub-zero weather, the fierce wind and bitter cold were so overwhelming, that the words of the prayers could not be enunciated properly. During the recitation of the 23rd Psalm, instead of saying: "Though I walk through the valley of the shadow of death", the following came out: "Though I walk through the SHALLEY of the VADOW of death." Fortunately, because of the intense wind and freezing temperature, no one was listening attentively except for the funeral director. He looked at me in wonder. Realizing my error I tried to correct myself! The more I tried, the more jumbled the words emerged... I finally gave up. Score: Cold 1- Karzen 0 !

Funeral Melodies

A first year cantorial student, a close friend of a bereaved family, was requested to co-officiate with me at a funeral service. Meeting in the chapel lobby, I asked the young novice which of the T'hillim (Psalms) he wished to chant. The budding cantor admitted that he knew none of the psalms, but was prepared to sing one of two selections in honor of the deceased. He had brought the sheet music to "Eli Eli" (Yiddish folk song) and "Kol Nidre." (prayer from the liturgy of the Yom Kippur Eve service) Which did I think was most fitting and appropriate? As to the traditional Memorial Prayer—El Malay Rachamim—and Psalms—they didn't learn that until the second semester!

The Cantor does a Shereleh

The following story did not actually happen to me, but I include it because I know it to be true.

My rabbinic colleague was to preside at two funerals within an hour and asked his Cantor to go to the cemetery after funeral #1 and conduct the burial ceremony. The inexperienced cantor had never before officiated alone at an internment and was nervous and reluctant to assume this task. The Rabbi carefully wrote out the exact procedure to follow. He included the custom following the closing of the grave, when friends are requested to form the traditional SHURAH, the double line for the mourners to walk through, receiving words of condolence .

The burial service proceeded without a flaw. The Cantor was a true professional! That is… until the very end. Without thinking, he confidently announced: "Ladies and Gentlemen..the service has been completed. Will everyone now form a double line so that we can do a SHERELEH." (Traditional Jewish folk dance).

Al & Millie Ruderman

A lady once inquired as to why, during the traditional Memorial Prayer for the dead, in addition to the specific name of the departed loved one, the Cantor always adds the names of Al and Millie Ruderman!

"Who are they, that their names are always included? Some special saintly couple?"

The prayer referred to was the "El Malay Rachamim" (God, Full of Compassion...).

This woman, as she listened to the Cantor chant the opening words, did not hear EL MALAY, but heard Al and Millie. Instead of RACHAMIM, her ears heard Ruderman.

Father and Son do the Sunday Cemetery Circuit

One beautiful Sunday morning my six year old son asked to go along on what was traditionally a Rabbi's busiest day of the week. A good bonding opportunity.

That particular day, I had to travel to three different cemeteries around the Chicagoland area to conduct eight monument unveilings. Uri promised to behave and stand aside quietly while the service was being conducted. He enjoyed driving with me as we made our way from cemetery to cemetery.

On Monday, the teacher asked each child to share what they did over the weekend. Our son proceeded to give a blow by blow description of the various cemeteries, the names of each, where they are located and what transpires at dedications. A stunned teacher called that afternoon to inquire if this was a regular occurrence and suggested that this was a bizarre activity for a young child!

P.S. His classmates wanted to join me the following week!

Believe it or not Funeral Tidbits

The following humorous tidbits are all true:

1) Waiting for a graveside funeral service to begin, an impatient non-sophisticated mourner insisted that we wait no longer for latecomers and exclaimed: "Let's get this show on the road."

2) A husband wanted me to either sing or recite the words to the popular song "Red Sails in the Sunset" as part of the funeral service..... because it was his wife's favorite song.

3) A daughter insisted on placing a telephone in the casket of her mother so that their daily conversations could continue even after death. (I always wondered what would happen if such a phone was installed and then it rang! Or what if the daughter called and the line was busy? And would these be long distance or local calls?)

4) A wife was crying bitterly at the casket of her husband. She

was hysterical— weeping and moaning about her loss and how she would be unable to carry on and cope without him. In her grief she screamed out to God: "How could you do this to me?" And then as she turned to take her seat in the chapel, she paused, looked at the Talit draped casket and said: "OKAY, Moshe, ZY GEZUNT!" (Be Well)

The Family Feud: "Rabbi! Do Something!"

On one occasion it was my sad role to preside over a double funeral: Two men had been brutally murdered in their place of business during a robbery—a father and son-in-law.

Evidently there were many serious problems in the family circle before this tragedy occurred. The sight of two caskets brought out the hidden hostility and deep anger and a major fight erupted minutes before the funeral was scheduled to begin. The caskets were pushed, the flowers toppled, chairs overturned. The police had to be called to intervene and restore calm.

Meanwhile as the pushing, shoving and name calling was at its peak, someone yelled: "Rabbi, Do Something!" I immediately began reading the Psalms and that seemed to have a calming effect. Before the police arrived, everyone was seated.

Never question the power of prayer!

The White Envelope

A sobbing lady called to inform me that her husband had just passed away. She invited me to officiate and eulogize her late husband. She had heard about me from friends and wanted me to know that I came highly recommended. She wanted a beautiful "send off" and memorable funeral service for her husband.

I was flattered. She then quickly added: "I know that you are a fancy suburban Rabbi. Please realize that I am a simple lady of modest means and cannot afford the high honorariums that you are used to receiving."

I assured her not to worry about the rabbinical fee. We agreed to meet an hour before the funeral in order visit with members of the family and acquire information about the deceased for the eulogy.

Upon entering the chapel, I could not help but notice the very ornate wooden casket. The funeral director confirmed that this certainly was not a charity case and the deceased was being given a "royal" send off.

Following the service, the widow approached me in the vestibule and praised me for the beautiful ceremony and handed me the famous "white envelope" containing the rabbinic honorarium. I normally don't open such envelopes in the presence of the family, but my curiosity forced me to do so. Inside was a twenty dollar bill. I just stared but did not say a word!

Upon arrival at the cemetery, the widow approached me and said: "I could see that you weren't happy with what I gave you, so here is something extra." She pressed crumbled bills in my hand. The burial was completed and upon returning to my automobile I discovered that she had given me an additional five one dollar bills!

When I visited the family during the Shivah (the week of

mourning), the widow had already set the date for the unveiling of the monument and invited me to conduct this consecration of the Matzeva (monument). With consistency, I received twenty five dollars for this second service also.

A few years later she also died. The chapel called me to officiate at her funeral. But this time, the funeral home paid all the bills from her estate and I was properly compensated for my time and efforts.

The Taxidermist Request

A young resident of a nearby community suddenly died and the hysterical wife called for me to come and help them with the funeral arrangements. Entering the home, I discovered that the deceased was lying on the living room couch.

After my opening words of comfort and condolences, as I preparing to explain the necessary procedures that must be immediately attended to, the woman defiantly said: "I do not wish to bury my husband...I want you to recommend a Jewish Taxidermist. I intend to have my husband stuffed and remain here lifelike on the couch, where he always rested and watched television. He will then always be with me."

After the initial shock, I proceeded to explain that there are state and local laws—not to mention Jewish law—which prohibit doing this. A proper burial is required according to our religion.

Disappointed that I wasn't going to agree to her request, she announced that she would consult with a less religious Rabbi, who might be willing to accede to her desire to have her husband stuffed for posterity. Obviously, she could not find any Rabbi who would agree to her outrageous, illegal, unrealistic request.

The husband was eventually buried according to Halacha (Jewish law). To this day, every time I pass a taxidermy shop or see a mounted animal or fish on a wall, I have visions of this chap hanging in the den of their home. May his memory be for a blessing!

Just Me at the Unveiling

I once officiated at the funeral of a woman whose entire family lived on the West Coast. While the family did travel to Chicago to attend the funeral, a few months later the following message was received:

"We are unable to return to the Midwest for the unveiling of a monument to our beloved mother. Enclosed please find a check for your professional rabbinic services for the ceremony of the Monument dedication. The stone is already in place. We are requesting you to go to mother's grave at your convenience and conduct a proper dedicatory service. Recite the appropriate Psalms and prayers. Please also say a few words in tribute to mother, even though no one will be in attendance."

And so it was done. The following day I visited the grave site and recited the traditional words and chanted the El Malay Rachamim prayer. I even delivered a brief inspirational message about the deceased, as would have done, had the family been present.

It was a strange feeling standing and speaking to no one. The Jewish mother buried in that grave was entitled to a Kosher bonafide ceremony. I know she was listening!

How Many Make a Minyan?

The most memorable unveiling story.......

While it is not required to have a Minyan (quorum of ten men) at an unveiling, it is nevertheless desirable, so that the Mourner's Kaddish can then be recited at the grave. The recital of this prayer requires a quorum of ten adult male Jews!

On one occasion, we had to wait for the "tenth man" to arrive.

Mingling with the small group, I discovered that one of the guests present was a non-Jew. The latecomer, for whom the family was waiting, finally arrived. Not wanting to embarrass anyone with the fact that a non-Jew cannot be included in the minyan, I quietly suggested that we wait another few minutes—perhaps another unexpected male might happen to arrive. The son of the departed counted and was a bit puzzled by the need for an eleventh male. He turned and remarked: "You know, this is the first time I realized that a Rabbi isn't counted into the minyan!"

Decades later I was relating this story around the Shabbat table in the home of friends in Jerusalem and the host told us that he could top this story!

Our friend was attending a business meeting in a Manhattan office building. Realizing that the hour was late, he began to leave in search of an afternoon "Mincha" (name of the traditional afternoon prayers) service in order to recite the Kaddish (prayer recited by a mourner) in observance of a Yahrzeit. (anniversary of death of a departed loved one)

The client offered to arrange for a minyan in his office by recruiting the required ten men from the building. There would be no need to rush away. Within minutes a quorum appeared—but one of the men was clearly not of our faith. In the spirit of brotherhood, a non-Jew had volunteered to join the minyan, wear a skullcap and accept the small prayer book that was supplied.

Not wanting to embarrass anyone, our friend suggested that they get an extra man. Why the need for an eleventh man? Thinking fast, he replied: "Because today is Rosh Chodesh!"—(the first day of a new Hebrew month)

And so it was—an eleventh man was summoned and the service recited and the Yahrzeit duly observed. The next morning the client called his friend and wanted him to know what an honor it was for him to have hosted the Mincha service in his office. "That's what I like about you Orthodox Jews! You know the finer points of Jewish law and even the special occasions when you need eleven men for a minyan. We non-Orthodox don't know these bits of trivia. Our Rabbi never taught us these technical rules." A true story!

Editor's note: If you would need "11" for a minyan on Rosh Chodesh, would you need "12" in months with a two day Rosh Chodesh observance?

This is my Shul Because....

The Congregation had succeeded in building a House of God! With a moving, dedicatory ceremony, that included a colorful parade escorting the Torah Scrolls to their new home; a new glorious chapter began.

Maine Township Jewish Congregation Shaare Emet (Gates of Truth) had a permanent address and I finally had a real office! Most importantly, the Jews of Des Plaines had a place to point with pride and say: "This is my Shul! (Synagogue)"

Not infrequently did the office receive a call from a local hospital informing us that a member of the Synagogue was a patient and would very much appreciate a pastoral visit from the Rabbi. Often the roster did not show such a member. When I visited the hospitalized individual, they would invariably tell me that they consider my Synagogue as their own because:

(a) They live nearby
(b) They drive by and regularly read the outdoor bulletin board
(c) This is the Synagogue they would join if they ever did affiliate with a Synagogue
(d) They have friends who belong and they say such nice things about the Shul family
(e) They once attended a Bar Mitzvah in the Sanctuary
(f) They vote in the building—(our Synagogue had become the neighborhood polling station on election days)
(g) They once purchased an item from the Sisterhood Gift Shoppe
(h) They play Bingo in our building.
(i) They once attended the Men's Club Las Vegas Night
(j) They attended, as a guest, a Sisterhood fashion show
(k) They once dropped in during our annual Auction
(l) They thought of once attending an adult education class
(m) On Yom Kippur they attended the "freebie" Yizkor Memorial Service.

The Synagogue Janitorial Staff

1) The Shul had a most wonderful Italian Catholic janitor/maintenance man. He wasn't religious and seldom attended church, but he did listen to our services regularly and never missed a Friday Night sermon. He used to repeat my Dvar Torah (Torah thoughts) to his religious Catholic wife and children at their Sunday family dinner. Many times he would comment that when he died he wanted me to eulogize him, because I knew him and understood him better than his parish priest. And he was probably right!

However, when he died, the family insisted that their priest deliver the eulogy. Attending the funeral, the family requested that I be one of the pallbearers! It was an honor to do so and have always considered it a Kiddush Hashem! (Sanctification of God's Name)

2) His replacement was a Seventh Day Adventist who would not work on Shabbat. He sent a friend to handle the Sabbath details. What a unique experience to have a non-Jewish "Shomer Shabbat" (Sabbath observer) on the staff. Each day he brought a question about the Bible. Jokingly, I would comment to my officers, how I longed for the time when Board members would also ask an occasional question about a perplexing verse they read in the weekly portion. I also yearned for the time when my membership would be as serious about the Shabbat as was our new maintenance man. It never happened!

The Only Rabbi in History to be Thrown out of Saks

How does a nice, sincere Rabbi get to be thrown out of the elegant Saks Fifth Avenue emporium (Lingerie Department) in the Old Orchard Shopping Center in Skokie, Illinois, while trying to do a Mitzvah? A bizarre happening, but true!

A new male member of the Congregation called one day to announce that he is engaged and invited me to officiate at the marriage in a few months. A Simcha! (A joyous occasion) I love a Simcha!

During the premarital interview, I discovered that the prospective groom had been previously married— and had no Gett. He had a civil divorce, but never obtained a Jewish divorce. At the time of the civil divorce neither he nor his wife were planning to remarry.. Had this couple been a member of my flock I would have insisted on the Jewish divorce immediately to prevent problems that often arise when this ritual is delayed

I called the "ex" to request her presence at the Jewish Ecclesiastical Court (Bet Din). She wasn't anxious to cooperate since it meant being absent from work. She saw no necessity after four years to fulfill this obligation. Afterall, she wasn't getting married!

Following a lengthy persuasive conversation, she finally agreed that the Rabbinic Court could issue the Gett. She would receive it through the "Shliach" procedure. I would be the agent and deliver it to her! She did not want to confront her former husband.

The lady was not told that her ex-husband was about to be remarried.

The Gett was written and the court appointed me to deliver this document. Now time was of the essence. The wedding was scheduled and all that remained was for the ex-wife to hold the Gett in her hands for a few seconds in the presence of two witnesses.

I called her to set up an appointment and was even willing to come to her apartment with the two witnesses. She began to get suspicious. The Rabbi was pushing too hard.

Why the sudden rush? She put two and two together and suddenly realized that the "ex" was probably planning to remarry. She now had a change of mind and would not cooperate and accept the Gett.

What was I to do? Only days remained before the wedding and the pressure was building. This crisis called for rabbinic ingenuity.

The "divorcee" worked as a saleslady in the lingerie department of Saks Fifth Avenue. Devising an ingenious plan, I enlisted the help of two colleagues: the Cantor and the Educational Director! They reluctantly agreed to be my witnesses.

The plan: They would stand at the entrance of the store and I would pretend to be shopping for a gift for my wife. Certain that the saleslady would not recognize me, since she was not a member of my Synagogue, I approached the counter with the Gett hidden in my coat. Before I had a chance to even ask her to show me some of the lovely merchandise, she began screaming for the manager and accused me of harassing her. She obviously did recognize me!

Promptly, I was expelled from Saks with a stern warning never to again come into their shop or they would call the police and have me arrested. The Cantor and Principal had already disappeared and I was left alone in defeat. It was, as you can imagine, a very embarrassing moment in my rabbinic career.

The wedding took place without me under the canopy. The couple understood and sympathized with me. Another Rabbi was recruited. The Gett was never delivered!

Never again have I entered Saks First Avenue. But it was their loss, not mine. Subsequent gifts to my wife were purchased at other fine shops. I estimate Saks' loss to be in the hundreds of dollars.

Jews by Choice Stories

Seldom did a week pass without a frantic call from a distraught parent inquiring about whether I might be available to teach a non-Jewish person for the purpose of conversion to Judaism. In most cases their adult child was romantically involved and very much in love with someone not of our faith.

While I did everything possible to discourage conversion for the sake of marriage and often succeeded in having the couple re-evaluate their relationship, I did accept a number of students for possible conversion if I felt they were truly sincere and would be an asset to our people.

Some of the students rightfully dropped out before completion of the course, because they were intellectually honest enough to admit that they could not live a Jewish lifestyle. Others completed the courses and were accepted as righteous converts. (Gerim)

I could share many stories about this conversion phenomenon.

Let me cite two, which could be called a BITTERE GELECHTER (funny if they wouldn't be so sad) ... 1) Each convert understands that he/she must, in principle, agree to be an observant Jew. While we cannot realistically expect each Ger (convert) to observe all of the 613 commandments, there are some Mitzvot which are nonnegotiable—i.e. Sabbath observance, Kashrut, (Dietary Laws) etc. Another basic Mitzvah which was expected of every student, was to agree that after their marriage, when they would be blessed with male children, to have a Kosher Circumcision/Brit Milah (Ritual Circumcision) by one of the certified Mohalim (clergymen who are trained and licensed to perform the Brit).

A sincere young lady converted and made the required pledges and commitments to live an Orthodox lifestyle. I solemnized the marriage to her Jewish boyfriend and within a year she was the new mother of a healthy baby boy. The proud father called me to announce the birth of their first male son.

I volunteered to help arrange the Brit for the following week. How shocked I was to hear the young father tell me that HIS family had decided not to have the traditional Brit so as not to impose the necessity of a large party on the new parents. By having a doctor do the circumcision in the hospital on the third day, the baby could come home already healed from this minor operation. A low key kind of circumcision!

Furious, I told the new father that his wife has pledged before a Bet Din of three Orthodox Rabbis at the Mikveh (ritual bath), that if and when she would be blessed with a male child she would agree to have a Kosher Brit Milah on the eighth day and by a Mohel.

His reply shocked and disappointed me. He said that his wife had to agree to say this or otherwise we would not have converted her. He added that everyone knows that converts make many promises but do not really intend to follow all of the teachings, once the conversion ceremony is completed.

Now I was even more furious and felt betrayed by my student, in whom I had invested many months of intensive teaching. She had deceived me!

"I am compelled to annul your wife's conversion retroactively," I defiantly stated. "I will convene the three Rabbis who signed her conversion certificate under deception and publish the retraction of the Gerut (Conversion) in the local newspaper!" "You can't do that," he insisted.

"Then read tomorrow's Chicago Sun-Times," I retorted, as I hung up the phone.

Five minutes later the paternal grandfather was on the phone. "Rabbi, I understand from my son that you are overreacting and threatening our family!"

I calmly responded that after spending countless hours and many months preparing his daughter-in-law to become Jewish, she did not fulfill her promise to have her son brought into the Covenant of Abraham, as required by our Torah.

Furthermore, I added, I am disappointed that the members of the family did not understand how crucial this major Mitzvah is to our religion. I continued to rebuke the new Saba (grandfather) and reminded him that he was supposed to be a role model for his new Jewish daughter-in-law. Because of me, he now had a Jewish grandson and I expected some Jewish loyalty from the new grandparents.

Finally, he blurted out: "Okay, Rabbi, we'll do it your way". "It's not MY way," I reminded him, "its thousands of years of the Jewish way!"

The Brit Milah was done properly on the eighth day by a Mohel. The Seudah (feast) was Kosher and a month later the Pidyon Haben was performed K'dat V'kdin. (according to strict religious observance)

At the Pidyon Haben the grandfather took me aside, hugged and kissed me. He thanked me for making him realize and be aware of his obligation towards being an inspiration and mentor to his children. He promised that he would make every effort now to fulfill his duty properly as a Jewish father/father-in-law and grandfather.

Score: Judaism 1 Ignorance 0

(2) The second episode...

An intelligent, beautiful Christian lady came for an interview about conversion to Judaism. As I suspected, she was in love with a Jewish man from our community. I accepted her as a student on condition that her boyfriend attend all of the classes with her. This was my policy—each candidate that had a Jewish "significant other" had to attend the sessions together.

The young lady read book after book on Judaism and absorbed

the material she read as well as the information taught to her. She asked penetrating questions and was eager to be exposed to everything Jewish. She attended Shabbat services, attended Judaic lectures in the community and was a model student. A budding ideal convert!

One day she came to me puzzled and disturbed. She had just met her future mother-in-law and they had a lengthy visit together. This Jewish mother evidently proceeded to give misinformation regarding Judaism, distorting our religion and undermining my carefully planned educational program.

Among the items my student revealed, that she heard from her future mother-in-law:

a) Judaism is a "pick and choose religion"—you have the option to select which Mitzvot to observe and to discard those that are not to your liking....

b) You aren't expected by the Rabbis to observe a maximum of the commandments. Because you can pick and choose, you have the flexibility to observe those commandments that are easy and not too time consuming...

You can keep a Kosher home, but eat anything outside the home.

d) Candle-lighting need not be done every week... Only on special Sabbaths and the IMPORTANT Jewish holidays.

My student asked correctly: "You taught me that Mitzvot are obligatory. They are commandments and not merely suggestions" (she had well remembered one of my pet sayings).

I didn't want to hear anymore... Livid, I asked her to leave the rest to me.

The boyfriends family was immediately summoned for a consultation meeting. I always met with the prospective Jewish family to give a progress report and update them on the conversion candidate.

The family was unaware of the meeting with the student or that she had told me of the conversation which had transpired earlier.

I proudly boasted of the progress made to date with my special student. They were happy to hear these words and the smiles on their faces expressed the Nachas they were feeling.

At that point I began to use the very words the mother-in-law had used...

"Judaism, you know, is not a 'pick and choose' religion...Every Jew is expected to observe a maximum amount of Torah law—not as little as you can get away with... Being a Jew means making a commitment to try and add as many Mitzvot into your repertoire as is possible."

I specifically singled out candle-lighting that was to be religiously performed EVERY Sabbath and holiday eve, Kashrut observance inside and outside the house... and finally I asked the new in-laws to make a commitment to start adding Mitzvot into their lifestyle so as to be genuine role models and an inspiration to my student.

Emphasizing that after she completed her studies and undergoes the conversion ceremony, the Rabbi's role has officially ended, but "yours is just beginning."

They listened in shock. But they soon realized that if the Gerut (conversion) was to be more than merely symbolic, they had to create a Jewish home for her to have the reinforcement that every convert needs (and alas doesn't always get.)

A promise was made that candles would be kindled in their home weekly. They further promised that they would also study and start adding more tradition into their lives.

The conversion took place. The wedding was magnificent. The children now attend Jewish Day School!

Score: Judaism 2 Ignorance 0.

Gerut (Conversion) Nachas Notes

1) Two of my female converts who had originally converted to marry Jewish spouses eventually divorced their husbands, because the men were not at all interested in following a Jewish lifestyle.

One husband insisted on violating the laws of Shabbat and Kashrut and a second bride confided that her husband refused to consent to the observance of Taharat HaMishpacha (Laws of family purity that govern sexual relations between husband and wife).

Both are now happily married to husbands who are practicing Orthodox Jews!

2) One of my male converts, of whom I was always so proud, has even become a Rabbi! A real Nachas (pleasure) Note! Though he is not an Orthodox spiritual leader, he is an outstanding pastoral Rabbi to his flock; to the infirm as a hospital chaplain; to the military establishment as a Navy Chaplain. A very special person!

"Selling" the First Born Sons

For Passover to be properly observed, it becomes necessary to "sell" all leaven products to comply with the Biblical command which prohibits ownership of "Chametz" (leaven). Each Rabbi, acting as an agent for his members, has a special form which authorizes the Rav (Rabbi) to handle this sale to a non-Jew on the eve of Pesach. (Passover)

Additionally, there is a long standing tradition for all first born sons to fast Erev Pesach, in gratitude that the Jewish Bchorim (first born sons) they were spared during the tenth and final plaque in Egypt before the Exodus. By attending a special

"Siyum" ceremony in the Synagogue to share in the completion of a tractate of Talmud (encyclopedia of the Torah), the attendee is exempt from fasting.

Each year, during the busy week before Yom Tov (term noting a major holiday), a wonderful, devout Savta (grandmother) would come to my office to "sell" her first born! She came with a list of four names for me to sell—her own first born and also the names of her three daughter's first born.

She insisted, despite my explanation that we (a) sell Chametz and (b) the first born fast on Passover Eve, that in her family the custom is to SELL the first born. She watched as I wrote these names on my Selling of Leaven forms.

She has since passed away and I am told that her grandchildren now follow their grandmother's tradition. They, too, go to their respective Rabbi each erev Pesach to sell their first son, as they were taught by the matriarch of their family.

An exaggerated example of the principle "Minhag Avotaynu Byadenu" (the customs of our parents must be maintained) and the verse from Proverbs 1:8 "Al Titosh Torat Imecha." (Do not forsake the teachings of your mother)

When Do Services Begin?

To have a Bar or Bat Mitzvah at Maine Township Jewish Congregation was a special Simcha. This was the home of "Joyous Jewishness" and everyone attending a celebration in our Sanctuary hopefully came away feeling uplifted and inspired.

Some referred to us as a Bar Mitzvah Factory, but each Shabbat, hundreds of worshippers attended our Tefilah (prayer service). Most were guests of the weekly Bar Mitzvah family- a captive audience forced to share a few hours of the Joyous Jewishness service at MTJC Shaare Emet. (Gates of Truth)

We would receive phone calls during the week inquiring as to the exact time the Bar Mitzvah was scheduled to "go on." The invitation each guest received stated when the service commenced, but not what time the Baal Simcha (celebrant) would do "his thing."

The non-Jewish invitees were the first to arrive for services and often preceded the host family. The Christian guests didn't want to miss even the opening blessings! On the other hand, the Jewish family and friends would invariably stroll into the Synagogue throughout the morning. Morning prayers and the Torah reading were not always a priority. Everyone knew that the "Bar Mitzvah part" occurred at 11 AM....and at that magic hour the Synagogue was always SRO.

The Sermon Sleeper

The purpose of the sermon is to teach and inspire! It has to be stimulating, thought-provoking and touch the heart and soul of the congregants. My aim was, that after services people would discuss, argue with and even challenge me. But above all, no one would sleep during these often controversial, but relevant sermons.

Though I boast that no one ever slept during my sermons, there was one exception— a regular member of our Minyan who ALWAYS slept during the sermon! He never missed a Shabbat service and each week when I rose to address the flock it was time for him to slumber.

This fine, sincere gentleman had a serious insomnia problem. For some strange unexplainable reason, only when I spoke could he relax and go into a deep sleep.

It would not have been so noticeable had he not snored. This became a problem and the Ritual Committee called a special meeting in order to find a solution to this embarrassing situation.

It was decided that he be made to change his seat. He had always gravitated to the front rows, unlike many others, who love to sit in the rear of the Sanctuary. Our friend was told that, for his own sake, to avoid the embarrassment and laughter that accompanied his snoring, he should sit in the rear area of the Shul.

Furthermore, it was decided that while he may sleep during the Rabbi's sermon, snoring would not be tolerated. Should he begin snoring, he would immediately be awakened by an usher who was assigned to stand nearby.

Eventually our insomniac member moved away and we lost a worshipper. We all missed him. He added a bit of color to the Minyan. Gone was that distinctive dulcet tone when he began to snore. He was probably the only worshipper in history who hoped the Rabbi's sermon would be longer! I fondly remember him to this day and am proud that I fulfilled my pastoral role towards him by giving him the opportunity to sleep for 20 minutes each Shabbat morning.

The Saga of Page 335

An estimated 100+ guests joined us each Shabbat as invitees of the Bar Mitzvah family. Often, many of them were unfamiliar with the prayer book and with formal Synagogue worship. It was necessary to have English during the Tefilah and to regularly announce the page in the Siddur.

The usher at the entrance of the Sanctuary warmly greeted each guest, handed him/her both a Siddur and Chumash (Bible) and told the page number that we were currently reading.

On one occasion our dedicated chief usher was discharging his obligation with zeal, handing out the books to a group of latecomers. He announced:" 335 " Whereupon one of the guests reached for his wallet, took out a $5 bill and said: "I hope you have change!"

The Bigger the Better

One Shabbat, a guest was not satisfied with the regular sized Bibles that were being distributed. He requested a more "Orthodox" edition. The good hearted usher rushed to me on the Bimah (pulpit) and asked if we had a larger sized volume to give to this gentleman. I, too, was impressed to have such a visitor in the Congregation, who obviously wanted to utilize the Torah Service to peruse the various standard commentaries that are found in the comprehensive editions of the Bible.

I happily gave my own personal edition to the usher, who proceeded to deliver it to the guest.. Ten minutes later I noticed that this man had come to Shul with a magazine. He had opened the larger Chumash and "hid" the magazine inside the "big book." Now he could relax and read his favorite magazine without anyone noticing. He had tuned out the service and was absorbed with his reading material. With our smaller editions of the Bible he couldn't hide his contraband. A scholar he wasn't, but cunning like a fox he certainly was.

Non-Kosher Tape Recording

Shabbat was scrupulously observed in our Synagogue. Sabbath desecration was not tolerated. Obviously video or tape recording of the services were not permitted. One morning, a guest decided that she would tape the service by hiding the recorder inside her coat . Unfortunately for her she sat next to the Rebettzin. When Ruby saw what was happening, she quickly put an end to this desecration.. A new definition of a "shlimazal": trying to deliberately desecrate the Shabbat and unfortunately choosing a seat next to the Rabbi's wife!

Creative Hebrew (?) Names

The Congregation honored the Bar Mitzvah family each week with the majority of the Aliyot (Torah honors). A few honors were reserved for the regular Synagogue members who were obligated to be called to the Torah due to a Yahrzeit observance or special Simcha (joyous occasion i.e. baby naming or Ufruf—the pre marriage ceremony.)

A form was sent to each Bar Mitzvah family a month before their event. They were asked to consider carefully whom they wished to honor at the Torah service. Each family would fill out —in transliteration, if necessary—the Hebrew and English names of the honorees.

Families would submit the following:

1) Yogi Bear "HaKohen" (probably Yehuda Ber?) Kohen (A descendant of Aaron)
2) Shimma Bora (Shimon Baruch?)
3) Natalie (Naftali?)
4) Simpson (Shimshon?)
5) Mandel Bread (Mendel Ber?)
6) Sounds something like Gefilte Fish (it turned out to be Gedalya Fishel)
7) Sounds like Yiddishe Kup (best guess: Yehuda Koppel)
8) Sounds like Yankee Doodle (Yankel Dovid?)

9) Sounds like "He's A Sucker" (Yissacher!)
10) Pinky (Pinchas!)

A family added that one of their guests wanted us to know that he was a "LEFTY" (I think he meant to inform us that he was a "Levi"—a Levite— and entitled to the second Torah honor)

Even the Synagogue secretary became an expert with female names for the Mi Sheberach (literally: "May He Who Blessed"...) prayers for the sick. We received requests to pray for the following, who were ill, and needed a Refuah Shlema—(a speedy and complete recovery):

1) Mandel Bread (upon further investigation: Mindel Breindel)
2) Sorry Brine (obviously Sarah Breina)
3) Rugalach (we guessed Rachel)
4) Carmelcorn (Carmella?)
5) Sprinter (Shprintza?)
6) Milky Pishy (Malka Pesha!)
7) Chandelier (Shaindel?)

Hagbaah Lessons

A frantic call came from a gentleman who was invited to attend an upcoming Bar Mitzvah. He was asked by the family to accept the honor of lifting the Torah Scroll (Hagbaah) following the completion of the weekly reading. Unfortunately, he did not know what was expected of him. He explained over the phone that he was not a regular Synagogue attendee, had limited ritual skills but would appreciate if the Rabbi could spare a few minutes to teach him what and how to do this specific honor. He was in the neighborhood and could be in the office in minutes.

(Everyone has heard of the classic, perhaps apocryphal story, of the Jew who was given the honor of Hagbaah, lifts the Torah and in a loud voice, says: "What do I do with the damn thing now?" We did not want that to ever happen in our Synagogue!)

He arrived with two large Coke bottles! He had been told, evidently, that this honor involved lifting the Torah scroll. With a bottle in each hand we began practicing lifting an imaginary Torah Scroll. He "graduated" the "Coke" course and at the Bar Mitzvah, this student performed his honor like a pro! How proud he was and how much nachas his wife and children had that morning.

Everyone was talking about the Hagbaah! "Have you ever seen such a Hagbaah?' I was asked by the family. With a smile I replied that this was probably the finest Hagbaah our Shul had ever witnessed. (If only the Bar Mitzvah celebrant had practiced as much and as hard as this Hagbaah honoree.)

An apocryphal story is told of the man who was given the honor of lifting the Torah. He came to the Bimah for the Hagbaah and because of the unusually heavy Torah he almost dropped the Scroll. He lifted it properly but the unexpected weight caused him to lose his balance and his left hand and his right hand went in opposite directions and the Torah was almost dropped by this embarrassed gentleman.

He was determined never to have this happen again. So he practiced and practiced. He took Hagbaah lessons from his friends. He went to be tested by a Rabbi to assure that he was absolutely perfect.

A month later he attended the Synagogue again and was given a Torah honor. With confidence he ascended the Bimah, took the wooden handles of the Torah and with great skill lifted the Scroll. "How did I do this time?" asked the proud man. "You did great," replied the Gabbai, (one of the honor guards at Torah) "but you had Chamishi!" (Chamishi is one of the regular Aliyah (ascending the Bimah) honors requiring the honoree to recite a blessing but NOT lift the Torah Scroll.)

Accidents do Occur

Unpredictable events occurred over the years during Bar-Mitzvah services. On more than one occasion the celebrant fainted, either before he was called to the Torah or sometimes during the chanting of the Haftorah. (section from the Prophets following the Torah Reading on Sabbath and Holidays) At least twice, a frightened celebrant vomited. Countless times the shaking youngster spilled wine from the goblet while chanting the Kiddush. (Sanctification blessing over a goblet of wine) When the latter occurred, my comment would be that now I understand the meaning of the phrase in the 23rd Psalm "my cup runneth over." That would take the pressure off the embarrassed youngster.

How many times the celebrant had stomach pains and had to rush off the pulpit and disappear for, what seemed, forever. Had this happened during the service or even during the Torah reading, at least the service could continue. But what does a Rabbi do when it happens immediately before the Bar Mitzvah segment? And it did!

Who can forget the Shabbat when the paramedics were summoned. A guest had taken ill during the service and it always seemed to occur during the Bar Mitzvah and/or during the sermon! What Mazal! (luck) It never happened when the Cantor was chanting!

Exodus to the Restroom

Jewish guests who came early—obviously by accident— and were not used to a relatively lengthy Shabbat service invariably left the Sanctuary one or more times to go to the restroom. It is necessary to emphasize "Jewish" because non-Jewish guests sat respectfully during the entire service, always came on time, and did not intend to miss even one prayer of the service.

After many years of hosting so many Christians I came to the conclusion that non-Jews have stronger kidneys than Jews. They never have to disappear for lengthy periods during the Sabbath worship. An amazing unproved medical phenomenon!

A Noy or Goy

I experienced joy at presiding over thirteen hundred Bnai/Bnot Mitzvah during the years I served in the American Rabbinate. As I reflect upon those Smachot, many special moments linger in my memory.

Families occasionally requested that we allow an important guest or relative to chant the opening segments of the service. Often we had guests who chanted beautifully and enhanced the beginning of our service. Other times they angered our regular worshippers who resented such intruders, who massacred the Hebrew language and obviously had no ritual talent.

On one Shabbat, an amateur had been recruited by the family to lead us in the opening blessings. In his ignorance, he confused the letter NUN with the GIMMEL and proceeded to chant:... Baruch Atta..... Shelo Asanee "NOY"—(the word should be Goy). Praised be God who did not make me a "Goy." (a heathen)

Now just as during the Torah Reading, those who follow closely have no inhibitions about yelling out the correct word, a half dozen people, hearing this amateur Baal Tefilah sing "Shelo Asanee NOY," shouted out: GOY! GOY! After the service the man bitterly complained at the humiliation and abuse and how poorly he was treated. "Rabbi, Is this how guests are treated in your Congregation? You ought to be ashamed! Imagine, calling me a Goy!"

He was right. To embarrass another person is a major sin. The Ethics of the Fathers (3:15) states that "one who publicly embarrasses another human being has no share in the World to Come." We sent him a letter of apology with a copy to the family. From that time on, any guest who requested to lead us in prayer on a Shabbat had to first be auditioned by myself or the Chairman of the Ritual Committee.

"Shlepping" Nachas

The President of our Synagogue was always seated on the Bimah. It was an act of honor extended to the elected lay leader who gave so freely of his time, efforts, energy and talent.

It was the duty of the president to extend a Mazal Tov on behalf of the membership to the family each week and also to bestow upon the celebrant the official Bar Mitzvah certificate and a gift from the Congregation.

We had many presidents over the years. Each excelled in the responsibilities of their office and were remarkable. It is truly inspirational to contemplate the countless hours that were devoted to the Synagogue by this group of leaders.

One president would enjoy using the Yiddish expression, during his presentation, "Shlepp Nachas." He loved to say to each celebrant: "May your parents Shlepp Nachas from you!"

Many of us tried to respectfully suggest that the correct way of saying this is "Shepp Nachas." (May your parents experience true Jewish joy), but each week he insisted on blessing the celebrants by saying "May your parents Shlepp Nachas from you." The Yiddishists reading these words will understand the not-so-subtle difference between "shlepp" and "shepp." Many of our regular worshippers anxiously awaited his remarks each week because it provided a chuckle. Would he ever remember to correct his mistaken expression? He never did!

For two years he faithfully discharged his presidential obligation. Over 100 youngsters are today trying to fulfill his charge so their parents can "Shlepp Nachas." Most are already parents themselves and they, too, are starting to "Shlepp Nachas" from their own offspring.

To this day whenever someone uses the expression Shepp Nachas my wife and I always exchange smiles. Somehow I am so conditioned to the Shlepp Nachas blessing that when I hear it correctly said, I prefer my old president's Bracha.

Who knows! Maybe more parents should start "Shlepping Nachas."

Where is the Loyalty?

In addition to all of the above humorous episodes, one personal painful story cannot be forgotten. I prided myself on the fact that I never missed a Bar or Bat Mitzvah. The Bat Mitzvahs were always at the late Friday Night Family service. Often a Simcha in my wife's large extended family occurred in the city and I did not attend because we had one or more Bnai Mitzvah (plural for Bar/Bat Mitzvah) that weekend. She would go alone with the children and I would stay at home in order not to disappoint a member family who expected their Rabbi to officiate and preside at their milestone celebration and give a moving and memorable sermon.

My father died and was buried on a Friday afternoon in June 1979.

There was a Bat Mitzvah scheduled for that Sabbath Eve, the daughter of a long time member family. I was now in the midst of Shiva (the week of mourning), yet there is no mourning allowed by Jewish law on the Shabbat. Halachically, according to Jewish Law, I could attend and perform my rabbinic duties though my heart would obviously not be in it.

Because the family was so special and the celebrant a fine student in our Religious School, I ignored the advise of a number of officers, friends and family members and made the decision to conduct the Simcha, as if nothing personally had occurred in my own life that day. They had invited over a hundred guests. It was a very joyous, festive Simcha service in the finest tradition of our Joyous Jewishness philosophy.

The Bat Mitzvah family never found time to visit us during the week of Shiva.

Worse, before the High Holidays, when each family is expected to renew their annual Synagogue membership, they resigned! Why? Their last child had now been "Bat Mitzvahed" and they no longer needed our Synagogue. Consequently, why pay dues? Their affiliation was terminated.

Had I known that they were planning to leave the Synagogue family would I have still have presided during the Shiva week at their Simcha? The answer is obviously YES, but the pain of that experience lingers to this day! I never saw or heard from this family again. I have long since forgiven them, but the episode lingers in my memory to this day.

JME and the Power of the Mezuzah

By way of introduction to the following story, permit me to share this background with you. Ruby and I became involved in the Jewish Marriage Encounter experience. First as participants on a weekend retreat for happily married couples, in order to learn about better communication in marriage. We eventually became a rabbinic team couple and were part of the presenting couples who presided over these weekend retreats. These seminars were conducted in the Chicagoland area, but we also traveled to New York and California for these 2-day retreats.

We popularized such concepts as Couple Power, Couplehood, Togetherness, the idea of not being Married Singles after marriage, of spending quality time as a couple and always making time to be with one another.

Each couple is a TEAM (remember the first letters: Together Each Accomplishes More) and must strive to become Soulmates.

One of the major points was that while we have instant coffee, tea, soup and potatoes, there is no really instant success in a quality marriage. It often takes hard work to make a true marriage successful. While Judaism does teach that "Marriages are Made in Heaven" we didn't think it sacrilegious to amend it to read, "but the maintenance takes place right here down on earth."

On one weekend at the old Lido Beach Hotel in Long Beach, New York, a couple came to our room to discuss a major intimate crisis in their relationship. They were very much in love, but had no children after ten years of marriage. They had visited every medical expert and there was nothing physically wrong with either of them.

They wanted to know if there was some religious rite that might help her conceive.

Perhaps we might recommend a great Chassidic Rebbe to bless them. They were willing to try anything in order to become parents.

Remembering that the Lubavitcher Rebbe always recommended the checking of the Mezuzot when a major situation occurred in one's home, I asked as to whether they had checked their bedroom door Mezuzah lately? (handwritten parchment containing the Shma Yisrael prayer and encased on the doorpost) Shocked, the couple responded by admitting that they never knew a bedroom required such a religious artifact. They assumed that only the front and back door of the house needed this parchment.

I suggested that following this retreat weekend they purchase a Kosher Mezuzah for their bedroom. Further, I instructed them to always remember that God's presence is in that very private room and to think of Him when in the act of love making.

Within three months she became pregnant. After the birth of their firstborn daughter, the proud father called to ask my permission to allow them to name their child after me. While Ashkenazic tradition frowns upon naming a baby after the living, I was honored to have this child named in my honor. The naming of baby "Jane" (after Jay) took place in my Synagogue and today she, herself, is a mother.

On many occasions, I have related this story to demonstrate the power of the Mezuzah. This advise to childless couples has worked for many! On a lighter note, I have often remarked that in my capacity as a rabbinic marriage counselor, I have helped many women get pregnant—but not the way you think!

Rabbis Make Babies Like Everyone Else

Author Noah Gordon wrote a best seller entitled "The Rabbi". A neighbor, after reading this book, commented that for the first time she realized Rabbis are also human beings. She added that she could now visualize that rabbis indeed do have children the very same way, as laymen. How brilliant an observation!

The Frail Groom

Among the first services I had the pleasure of solemnizing was that of a beautiful senior citizen couple. Two families in the Congregation arranged this match between their respective widow/widower parents. It was to be a special Simcha. (joyous celebration)

The rather frail groom had just turned 80, and the bride was a few years younger.

He had been a professional football athlete in his younger years, but the years had taken their toll.

During the course of the ceremony, God's name was invoked asking Him to grant the bride and groom many more healthy years. As part of my standard opening English prayer, used during the ceremony, I added the word "strength"—that the Almighty should give this couple strength.

The groom responded, in a voice loud enough for all present to hear clearly: "Rabbi, I hope God hears your prayer!" Am I gonna need it tonight!"

Concentrated to Me

During the wedding ceremony, when the groom placed the ring on his bride's finger and recited that most crucial Hebrew statement:: Haray At Mkudeshet Li...(Literally "With This ring You Are Consecrated To Me." I always had the groom repeat the phrase also in English. It is Halachically important for the couple to both understand what is being said at that major moment in the ceremony.

The word "Mkudeshet" is usually translated as consecrated.

One groom was so nervous, as he stood under the Chuppah, he erred and said "With this ring you are CONCENTRATED to me as my bride..."

The assembled guests all chuckled as they listened to the bridegroom mispronounce the word. I seized the moment and immediately said to the embarrassed young man:

"In truth, your interpretation of Mkudeshet may be more correct. For what is marriage if not making the ultimate commitment to begin concentrating on each other! May you always concentrate on your partner, from this moment on, and truly become soulmates."

My Saddest Wedding

While most of the stories in this volume are (hopefully) humorous, there were occasionally sad episodes that remain with me.....

When a couple came for their pre-marital conference, the meeting would either generate positive or negative vibes in me. Somehow I could sense which of the brides and grooms were going to succeed and "live happily ever after" and which unions were on shaky ground.

One couple was already having a major disagreement before they entered my study.

During the course of our hour together, I sensed a serious crisis in their relationship. They didn't at all act like a loving couple and it was only a week before their marriage.

Knowing the parents of the bride, I made an appointment for the next day. They were somewhat aware of the rocky relationship, but ascribed it to the pressures, anxiety and excitement of the wedding. They brushed off my concerns and assured me that the couple loved each other and there was no reason to be concerned.

Upon arriving at the hotel to perform the ceremony, I was intercepted by the photographer. He wanted me to know that during the photo session there were disturbing signs atypical of a couple about to be married. It was even obvious to the photographer and the videographer.

This time I spoke with both sets of parents and suggested that maybe the marriage ought to be postponed. All four parents agreed that the Hawaiian honeymoon would resolve all the problems. They would be free of the pressures of the wedding and alone, together they would resolve their differences. Besides, "all the guests are here and the wedding is paid for!"

It was the saddest ceremony I ever performed. No one smiled. No one seemed happy! Not the bride and groom; not the parents.

Following the honeymoon trip the couple filed for divorce. The Gett was arranged with my assistance. Within two years, I had the joy of again officiating at two weddings to more suitable mates. Over the years I attended more than one Brit Milah and named their respective children.

RABBI JAY'S WORLD OF HUMOR 145

Squishing to the Chuppah

Many couples in America request the Rabbi to walk down the aisle as part of the official procession to the Chuppah. (bridal canopy) I always tried to accommodate the couple by leading the procession to the canopy.

One Sunday afternoon, the Chicago area was inundated with a major rainstorm. The excessive rains flooded the main roads near the hotel, where an elegant wedding was to be celebrated.

Because the roads were flooded, the police were rerouting traffic. Though the hotel was already visible, I was diverted in another direction. Car parking was finally found many blocks from the hotel.

Unprepared for this situation, I had to walk a quarter of an hour across streets that were literally under water. My shoes and socks were soaked, as were the bottom of my trousers.

The hour was late and there was no time to dry out. The

Ketubah (marriage contract) was signed, the Bedecken (veiling of the bride) had taken place and it was time for the processional to the Chuppah! Dressed in my white rabbinic robe and Talit, I began to walk down the aisle.

Squish! Squish! The combination of my soaked socks and shoes made an embarrassing noise as I began to approach the canopy—leaving wet footprints on the white runner. Normally the music would have drowned out the squishy sound, but for some reason these musicians opted to wait until I reached the Chuppah before commencing with the music.

What a nightmare! It seemed like eternity until I reached my place under the Chuppah. Every time I moved, I made strange, weird noises. It was all captured for posterity on the video. Decades from now their grandchildren will be viewing this Simcha and wonder where the grandparents found such a noisy Rabbi!

Boin

Perhaps my all time favorite classic story.

A prominent family came to see me with regard to their son's forthcoming Bar Mitzvah scheduled for the following season. The lad was about to begin his special private tutoring for the big event later that year The mother wanted her son to do more than merely the Maftir (final verses of the weekly Torah portion) and Haftorah. (Prophetic Reading) She asked if her son could also be taught by the Cantor to chant the "BOIN" part of the service.

"Boin?" I responded "What is Boin?" She insisted that her late mother had often remarked how wonderful it would be and how much more Nachas (joy) the family would realize if her grandson could do more than merely the expected minimum at the Shabbat worship.

"Before she passed on, Mother urged me to request that he be taught to do the Boin!"

Stumped again!

"Perhaps the departed had left this request in writing?" I asked.

"Yes," responded the woman in my office, "in fact, it is written in Hebrew."

I looked at the handwritten memo in her hand and on it was written the following word

$$\mathcal{P}_O I N$$

If you read the word as an English word from the left to the right, it does, indeed, look like BOIN... But if you read it as a Hebrew word, it spells out MUSAF, the name of the additional prayers recited on Sabbath and holidays. The elderly grandmother had wanted her precious grandson to serve as Baal Tefilla and chant Musaf prayers on his Bar Mitvah Sabbath.

The Bar Mitzvah celebrant was trained to chant Musaf, as was the last request of a proud grandmother. I am confident that from her place Above, she was having boundless Nachas listening to her grandson chant Musaf (or Boin!)

Rabbi Jay's Bar Mitzvah Day

We awoke to find the sun shining and the predicted rain not a reality. This was the big day. For the past thirteen years, since making Aliyah, Rabbi Jay had told the celebrants, that he felt reborn. Now that he was 13 years old should not the Bar Mitzvah King celebrate his own Simcha ? After all, important milestones such as birthdays and anniversaries are marked... why not Yom Aliyah? (The day that one "ascends" - moves to Israel)

The day went smoothly (as occasions organized through Rituals Unlimited do!)

As the celebrant was not from out of the country.......

The family was not a day late....
There were no lost luggage problems ....
There was no lost kid brother...
There was no lost kid sister ...
The mother did not forget her jewelry at home and thinking that the valuables were stolen, did not spend four hours filling out a police report (in Hebrew yet!)...
The father did not forget travelers checks at home and thinking that the checks were stolen .. finish from sentence above...
The family found the correct Kotel...
The hotel personnel did not forget to relate important messages from the Rabbi...
The father did not forget the "white envelope"...
There was no Uncle Dudu coming from Haifa, who was sure that he could complete the trip to Jerusalem, maneuver his way through the heavy traffic to the entrance of the city, enter the Old City, park the vehicle and walk to the Kotel, in no more than one hour. Of course, he misses the entire service!

The celebrant did not vomit from nervous tension...
The celebrant did not faint....
The celebrant did not leave his speech in the hotel room...

It was a wonderful day! The family and friends joyously prayed together, danced and sang at this very special service.
Of course, there was a party with a spiritual, Zionist twist to it. And a good time was had by all!

Eyewitness .. Ruby Ray Karzen (First wife)
Chanukah - December 1998

KARZENISMS

1) May God bless you ALWAYS--IN ALL WAYS!

2) Never boast that you are a GOOD Jew..because on the ladder of superlatives there is GOOD, BETTER and BEST. Good is the lowest level and there is no reason to be proud of being on the bottom the ladder. You may say: "I WAS a good Jew; but now I am a better Jew; some day I hope to achieve my Jewish Best!"

3) Being a Jew is an accident of birth. Make it the greatest accident of all time! More important than being a Jew by birth is to be a Jew by worth!

4) Living a Jewish lifestyle is a full-time job, not part-time. And as we all know, full-time pays better than part-time.

5) Some say that our religion is a religion of the past. I (partially) agree! Judaism is a religion of the past, but it is also a religion for the present and for the future.

6) Judaism is not a smorgasbord or a salad bar style religion, where you pick and choose which Mitzvah appeals to you at any particular moment. We have to accept the whole Torah as a package deal. We are expected to observe as many of the 613 Commandments as we possibly can, not as few as we can get away with.

7) The Almighty listens to all of the prayers we recite to Him... and he always ANSWERS them... But sometimes He says No!

8) Judaism is a "conversation between the generations" and its our obligation to guarantee that this ongoing conversation continues in our generation, so that we can assure that future generations will perpetuate the same conversation.

9) Every Jew should be a blend of the Orthodox, Conservative and Reform.

Orthodox means "right path" (from the Greek orthos doxo) and certainly every Jew should, indeed, walk in the right path; Conservative, because we have an obligation to assure that we conserve and save our beautiful traditions; Reform, because we need to reform those Jews who have gone astray.

10) Never say "I'm not religious!" Instead say, "I'm not religious YET!" Always add the word "yet!" You never know what might occur tomorrow. True, that today you are not observant. Something yet may happen tomorrow to change your life... and lifestyle.

11) It's fun to be a Jew! Approach each Mitzvah as it were a thing of Joy. Remember the words of the Psalmist: "Serve the Lord with gladness"... Remember and never forget....... "Joyous Jewishness!"

GLOSSARY

Acharon Acharon Chaviv--Last but not least
Adon Olom--Popular "God is Master of theWorld" hymn from the morning service
Ahavat Torah--Love of Torah
Ahavat Yisrael--Love of the Jewish People; Love for Israel
Ainikle--Yiddish for grandchild
Al Chet--Literally "For the Sin of".... Confessional prayer recited on Yom Kippur
Alenu--Closing prayer of the three daily services
Aliyah--Literally "to go up." Refers to (1) those who emigrate to Israel (2) one who ascends podium to have a Torah honor--Aliyah L'Torah
Amidah--Literally "standing." Refers to the most important prayer in the daily service recited in a standing position. This prayer is also known as the "Shmona Esray" (the number "18") because it originally consisted of 18 sections Amud--Podium from which the Cantor chants the prayers
Ani Maamin (Lit: I believe)--The 13 Principles of the Jewish Faith
Aseret HaDibrot--The Ten Commandments
Ashkenaz(ic)--Those Jews who descend from European stock and who follow specific ritual practices different from the Sephardim or Spanish/Portuguese background
Ashray--Name of one of the Psalms/prayers from the traditional morning and afternoon service (Literally "Happy"....)
Averah--Sin
Avirah--Atmosphere
Avodah--Section of Yom Kippur liturgy describing the Sacrificial ceremony
Ayn Kaylokaynu--(One of closing hymns from the morning prayers ("There is no one like our God")

Ayshet Chayil--Woman of Valor (Proverbs 31) recited at Sabbath Eve table
Azkarah--Graveside ceremony, usually on the Yahrzeit; memorial service
Baal Simcha--The celebrant
Baal Tefillah--Officiant at religious service; one who chants the prayers
Baal Koray--Designated Torah reader at Synagogue service
Baalagan--Hebrew slang for confusion & chaos
Bar Mitzvah--literally "Son of Commandment" but generally refers to the religious ceremony marking a 13 yr old male's entry into the adult Congregation; rite of passage celebrating his new status
Baruch Sheamar--Name of one of the traditional morning prayers (Literally: Blessed Be He Who Spoke)
Bat Mitzvah--literally "Daughter of Commandment", refers to the celebration marking a 12 year old female's new adult status.
Bchor--First born son
Bedecken--pre-wedding ceremony where groom places veil over bride's face
Bet Din--Rabbinic Court
Bimah--the podium or platform in the Synagogue from where the services are conducted
Birkat HaMazon--Grace After Meals
Birkat Kohanim--God's daily blessing through the Kohen to the Congregation
Bittere Gelechter--Yiddish expression (literally a "bitter laugh") meaning "It would be a laughing matter if it weren't so sad"
Bnai Mitzvah--plural form of Bar Mitzvah
Bnot Mitzvah--plural form of Bat Mitzvah
Bnei Brak--Israeli City near Tel Aviv dating back to Talmudic times
Bochur (or Bachur)--term to denote a male youngster, as in Bar Mitzvah Bochur; The Celebrant!

Bracha--A Blessing (i.e. over food or at the Torah) before performing a ritual commandment
Brachot--The plural form of Bracha--Blessings!
Brit Milah--Ritual Circumcision
Bubbe--Yiddish for Grandmother (Savta in Hebrew)
Challah--Sabbath/Holiday loaves of special twisted bread
Chametz--leaven (i.e. bread) products forbidden on Passover
Chamishi--the 5th of the traditional Torah honors on Sabbaths/Holidays
Chanukah--Popular 8 day minor winter Jewish holiday commemorating the rededication of the Temple in Jerusalem in 165 BCE., often spelled Hanuka.
Chanukat Habayit--Dedication ceremony for a new home
Charedi--(also spelled Haredi)- ultra Orthodox
Chassidim--(also spelled Hasidim) ultra Orthodox Jewish sect that originated in eighteenth century Poland and distinguished by their exclusive black garb and loyalty to a specific "Rebbe" (the loving term for their Rabbi)
Chazzan--Cantor
Chumash--The Five Book of Moses; the first section of the Bible or Pentateuch
Chupah--the bridal canopy under which a bride and groom stand during the marriage ceremony
Chupah-Kiddushin--The official marriage ceremony
Chiyyuv--Term used to denote one who is obliged to either chant the service or have a Torah honor (Aliyah) because of a Yahrzeit or other compelling reason (Plural: Chiyyuvim)
Darkay Shalom--Paths of Peace
Doven or Dovening--Yiddish for praying
Drasha--The Rabbi's Sermon (Dvar Torah)
Draydel--Yiddish for spinning top used during Chanukah week (Sevivon in Hebrew)
Dvar Torah--A "Word of Torah"; religious Torah thought or sermon delivered by Rabbi or any knowledgeable layman

El Al--The official Israeli government airline

El Malay Rachamim--"God is Full of Compassion"; The memorial prayer for the dead

Eli Eli--Yiddish folk song-"My God, My God, Why hast Thou forsaken me?"

Emunah--Faith and trust in the Almighty

Erev--Eve (of Shabbat or any holiday)

Farbrennt--Yiddish term referring to one who is "burnt" and zealous for a cause; totally consumed and committed to a particular cause

Farblongett--Yiddish expression for one who is lost, misguided, goes astray

Gabbai--The honored layman who stands as an honor guard at the side of the Torah reading table; Layman who appoints and distributes the various honors.

Gan Eden--Garden of Eden and used as euphamism for Paradise/Heaven

Ger--A convert to Judaism (pl: Gerim)

Gerut--(Giyur) Conversion

Gett---Jewish religious divorce; document written for a divorce

Glila--The honor of binding the Torah following the reading of the Scroll

Gomel--Blessing recited at Torah after recovering from serious illness, operation, trans-atlantic flight or a life threatening crises.

Goy--A non-Jew. Could also refer to a heathen

Haftorah--The chapters from the Prophets read at the Synagogue service after the Torah reading on Sabbaths and Holidays

Hadlakat Nerot--The candle-lighting ceremony on Friday and Holiday Evenings

Hagbaah--Ceremony of Lifting Torah for everyone to glimpse at the script Ashkenazim perform this act after the reading; Sefaradim before the reading

Hallel--Psalms of Praise recited on Rosh Chodesh and special holidays

Hashem--"The Name" (of God); term used to avoid uttering literal name of God

Hakafot--Circle dancing, usually with the Torah scrolls on Simchat Torah, but can also denote any dancing-i.e. round the Bar Mitzvah celebrant

Halacha--The body of Law that governs the Jewish way of life, comprising both the Written and Oral Torah (plural-Halachot)

Halavy--Yiddish for "were it only so"

Haray At Mkudeshet Li--Statement made at wedding cermemony by groom to his bride: "With this ring you are consecrated to me.."

HaMotzi--The blessing recited before eating bread

Hava Nagila--Popular Israeli folk song (literally: Come let us rejoice)

Hesped--Eulogy

Hotzaah & Hachnasah--Terms referring to the ceremony of Taking of the Torah from the Ark (Hotzaah) and the Returning of Torah to Ark (Hachnasah)

Hurva--The old great historic Synagogue (before1948) in the Jewish Quarter of the Old City of Jerusalem, now but a shell and popular tourist site

Kabbalat Shabbat--Evening service that ushers in and welcomes the Sabbath

Kaddish--The special prayer recited during period of mourning by the mourners and each year thereafter on the anniversary of the death of a close relative

Kal V'chomer--One of the 13 principles by which Jewish law is interpreted.

Kashrut--The Dietary Laws

Kdat V'Kdin--According to the strict letter of the law

Kavana--the devotion required by Jewish law for proper praying

Kavod--Honor

Ketubah--The marriage contract/document that is a part of every Jewish marriage.

Kibbudim--Honors (as distributed in the Synagogue)
Kibbutz--Israeli collective settlement
Kichel--Popular type of sugar cookie
Kiddush--Prayer of Sanctification over a goblet of wine recited at the Sabbath/Holiday able; also the refreshments following Shabbat/YomTov morning services
Kiddush Hashem--Sanctification of God's Holy Name (opposite term is Chilul Hashem-Desecration of His Name)
Kippa--Skullcap worn on the head by observant Jews (pl. Kippot) Yiddish term is Yarmulka
Kiruv--Concept of bringing people closer to Judaism through outreach
Knesset--Israel's Parliament, seat of government consisting of 120 members
Kohen--Descendant of Aaron and entitled to first Aliyah during Torah Reading
Kol Nidre--The Yom Kippur Eve service named for this prayer- "All vows"
Kol Bo--one who is multi-talented and can perform any and every ritual task
Korim--Prostrating on hands and knees before God during Alenu during the High Holiday Musaf liturgy and during Yom Kippur Avodah
Kosher--literally meaning "fit and proper", this term can refer to food that is permissible for Jewish consumption or to ritual objects, i.e. Torah Scroll , Tefillin or Mezuzah that are considered ritually acceptable and therefore allowed to be used to perform our religious obligations
Kotel--The Western Wall of the Holy Temple compound, holiest site in the Jewish world
Kovod--Honor (as in giving "kovod" to someone during services)
Kriah--Reading of the Torah; With different Hebrew spelling can also be the rending of a garment before a funeral
Kriat HaTorah--The Reading of the Torah at religious services

Kvell--To beam with delight
Lech Lecha--"Get Thee Out"; name of one Torah portion in the Book of Genesis
Levi--Descendant of Tribe of Levi (Levite); entitled to 2nd Aliyah at Torah Service
Lubavitcher Rebbe--One of the major Rabbis of the Chassidic Movement, named after Russian city of Lubavitch
Machzor--The High Holiday prayer book
Madrich--Tour guide; youth leader; camp counselor
Maftir--The final verses of the weekly Torah reading; the last Torah honor usually reserved for a prominent individual; almost always extended to a Bar Mitzvah celebrant (Maftir Aliyah) on a Shabbat or major holiday
Mandel Bread--Popular type of bakery delicacy
Masada--Historic mountain near Dead Sea
Matzeva--Monument/tombstone erected over grave
Mazal--Luck
Mazal Tov--Popular expression of Congratulations (lit: May you have good luck)
Meah Shearim--intensely Orthodox religious neighborhood of Jerusalem
Mechirat Chametz--Selling of leaven products to a non-Jew before Passover
Mechitza--the formal separation between the sexes at religious services usually by means of a physical barrier-i.e. fence, wall or balcony
Medinat Yisrael--The State of Israel
Mezuzah--The parchment containing the "Shma Yisrael" prayer inside a decorative case that is affixed to the right side of a door
Midrash--Rabbinic commentaries on the Scriptures
Mi Sheberach--prayer recited at Torah as blessing for those who have had an Aliyah; also a prayer recited at Torah for the sick and for naming a newborn girl

Minyan--Quorum of 10 males; minimal requirement for a public Synagogue service
Mishpacha--Family
Mitzvah--A Commandment! The religious obligations and duties of a Jew. (pl: Mitzvot) There are 613 Mitzvot in the Torah
Mohel--Ritually certified circumcision specialist who performs the Brit Milah
Musaf--The additional prayer service on Sabbath and Holidays
Nachas--joy, pleasure that every parent expects from children/grandchildren
Neilah--Closing service of Yom Kippur Day climaxing with the Shofar blast
Nes--A miracle (pl Nissim)
Netilat Yadayim--Ritual ceremony of washing the hands before eating bread
Nigun(im)--Traditional melody (melodies) chanted at services or sung at the Sabbath table
Noshery--snack food
Nudnik--Yiddish for a pest or an obnoxious person
Oneg Shabbat--Usually refers to a collation after religious services for socializing and camaraderie (literally Joy of the Sabbath)
Parshat HaShavua--Weekly Torah portion (often called The Parsha or Sedra)
PintelleYid--The spark within each Jew that can be ignited
Posek (pl. Poskim)--Great Rabbinic scholar/authority who renders Halachic decisions
Poskin--The Posek who decides Jewish law "poskens" (makes the final decision)
Proo Urvoo--The Mitzvah to be fruitful and multiply
Purim--Minor Jewish holiday-Feast of Lots- celebrating deliverance from attempted massacre of the Jews in ancient Persia
Ra'anana--Israeli city north of Tel Aviv
Rabbanit--Hebrew for Rabbi's wife (Rebettzin)
Rav-Rabbi

Rebbe--Usually refers to a Chassidic Rabbi
Rebettzin (Or Rabbanit)--Yiddish for Rabbi's wife
Rishon--First section of the Torah portion of week; First aliyah
Rosh Chodesh--The first day of the Hebrew month; a minor holiday
Rosh Hashanah--The Jewish New Year
Rosh Yeshiva--Head/Chief Rabbi of Rabbinical School
Rova--The Jewish Quarter of Jerusalem's Old City
Ruach--spirit (as in Sabbath Ruach/atmosphere)
Rugalach--type of traditional baked delicacy
Saba--Grandfather (Zayda)
Savta--Grandmother (Bubbe)
Saychel--Yiddish for "common sense"
Sefer Torah--TheTorah Scroll
Selichot--penetential prayers recited before and during the High Holiday season.
Semicha--Rabbinic ordination
Sevivon--Spinning top used during Chanukah holiday (Draydel in Yiddish)
Shabbat--(Shabbos)The Sabbath Day
Shachrit--Morning prayer service
Shalom Alayachem--Traditional Greeting; also name of hymn sung at Sabbath table
Shalom Bayit--tranquility in the home
Shayla uTshuvah--Questions/Answers in Halacha
Shehecheyanu--Special blessing recited on milestone occasions
Shekel (pl. Shekalim)--The official Israeli currency
Shereleh--Yiddish folk dance
Shiva--The 7 Day mourning period observed for deceased close relatives
Shepp Nachas--Yiddish expression for the hope that one will always experience Nachas from children & grandchildren
Shliach--Messenger; (i.e. the proxy who delivers a Gett to wife)
Shlimazzal--Yiddish for one who always seems to have misfortune befall him

Shma Yisrael--"Hear, O Israel" prayer recited twice daily and found inside the Torah (Deuteronomy) and in Mezuzot and Tefillin
Shockel--Yiddish for swaying during prayers
Shtetl--Yiddish for a small city
Shurah--Double row made by those attending burial service so mourners can pass through and receive the traditional words of comfort
Shva Na/Shva Nach--Technical grammatical terminology for correct pronunciation
Siddur--The Prayerbook
Sidra or Sedra--Torah portion of the week (same as Parsha or Parshat HaShavua)
Simcha--Joyous occasion (pl: Smachot)
Simchat Torah--Joyous holiday of Rejoicing with Torahs
Siyum--Completion of a volume of Talmud; refers to ceremony on morning of Passover eve, where the first born participate and are then absolved from fasting
Talit--prayer shawl worn during religious services by male worshippers (pl: Talitot)
Talmud--The encyclopedia explaining the Oral Law of the Torah.
Talmid Chacham--A scholar
Tefilah--Prayer
Tefilin--black leather phylacteries, containing chapters of the Torah, worn on the arm and head during weekday (never on Shabbat or major holidays) morning services
Tisha B'av--The Fast of the 9th day of Av to commemorate destruction of the two Holy Temples in 586 BCE and 70 CE
Torah--The Holy Scroll; The Five Books of Moses
Tzadakah--Charity
Tzitzit--the fringes that hang on the 4 corners of the prayer shawl
Vaetchanan--Name of Torah portion from Deuteronomy read following Tisha B'av

Yahrzeit--the annual anniversary observance of the death of a loved one

Yasher Koach--Literally "May your strength be upright" Popular expression used to congratulate someone following the performance of a religious ritual (i.e. Aliyah L'Torah or chanting Synagogue service); expression of appreciation; thank you

Yerushalayim--Jerusalem

Yeshiva--School of Higher education that trains students and future Rabbis

Yeshivat HaKotel--Famous Torah institution in Jerusalem's Old City

Yiddishkeit--Yiddish for Judaism and/or Jewishness

Yom HaAtzmaut--Israel Independence Day

Yom Kippur--The Day of Atonement

Yom Tov--A major Jewish holiday (lit: A good day)

Yom Tov Sheni (Shel Galiyot)--The extra day added to major holidays in the Diaspora

Zayda--Yiddish for Grandfather (Saba in Hebrew)

Zchor Briss (Brit)--Remember The Covenant; prayer recited during the pre-High Holiday "Selichot" (Penitential) Services

Zchut--A privilege or merit

Zman Kriat Shma--The (latest) time one is permitted to recite the "Hear O Israel" prayer

Zy Gezundt--Yiddish for "Be Well" (a blessing for good health)